PATTERNS OF HIGH PERFORMANCE

CONTACT INFORMATION:
JERRY L FLETCHER
415-456-5200
fletcher@hpdynamics.com
www.hpdynamics.com

PATTERNS OF HIGH PERFORMANCE

Discovering the Ways People Work Best

JERRY L. FLETCHER

Berrett-Koehler Publishers
San Francisco

Berrett-Koehler Publishers, Inc.
235 Montgomery Street, Suite 650
San Francisco, CA 94104-2916
Tel: (415) 288-0260   Fax: (415) 362-2512   www.bkconnection.com

Ordering Information
Quantity sales. Special discounts are available on quantity purchases by corporations, associations, and others. For details, contact the "Special Sales Department" at the Berrett-Koehler address above.

Individual sales. Berrett-Koehler publications are available through most bookstores. They can also be ordered directly from Berrett-Koehler: Tel: (800) 929-2929; Fax: (802) 864-7626; www.bkconnection.com

Orders for college textbook/course adoption use. Please contact Berrett-Koehler: Tel: (800) 929-2929; Fax: (802) 864-7626.

Orders by U.S. trade bookstores and wholesalers. Please contact Publishers Group West, 1700 Fourth Street, Berkeley, CA 94710. Tel: (510) 528-1444; Fax (510) 528-3444.

Berrett-Koehler and the BK logo are registered trademarks of Berrett-Koehler Publishers, Inc.

Printed in Canada

Library of Congress Cataloging-in-Publication Data
Fletcher, Jerry L.
    Patterns of high performance : discovering the ways people work best /
by Jerry L. Fletcher
        p.   cm.
    Includes bibliographical references and index.
    ISBN 1-881052-33-8 (hardcover : alk. paper) — ISBN 1-881052-70-2
(paperback)
    1. Employee motivation.   2. Achievement motivation.
3. Performance.   4. Psychology, Industrial.   I. Title.
HF5549.5.M63F58   1993
658.3'14—dc20   93-17921

First Hardcover Printing 1993
First Paperback Printing January 1995

09 08 07 06 05 04   10 9 8 7 6 5 4 3

Produced by Mary Carman Barbosa
Design: Beverly Butterfield
Copyediting: David Degener
Cover Design by Robb Pawlak

CONTENTS

PREFACE

If you have ever had the experience of trying to use someone else's process for succeeding, or trying to follow someone else's good advice about what you should do and found that you couldn't make it work, or, worse yet, wondering what was wrong with you that you couldn't, this book is for you. If you've been trained in a particular process for managing others or for selling a product, and you have wondered why, after laboriously learning the process, you find that you use very little of it in actual practice, this book will help you understand and respect your own wisdom in being selective. If your company has spent lots of money trying to identify the common characteristics of high performers in each of its critical job categories, then trained everyone to imitate them, and finds it now needs to follow the programs with something that recognizes individual differences, this book will explain what's missing.

This book will help you come to understand how unique and tightly integrated each person's success process is, including your own. Most advice and ideas from others will not work. Only the bits and pieces that reinforce your existing success process will actually be useful. Imitating other people's ways of doing something is only the first step toward achieving outstanding performance. This book is about the rest of the journey. Rather than berate yourself for your inadequacies, you need to respect your unique ways of doing things. To do that, you need to understand why they work the way they do. That understanding will put you in a position to guide the development of your own capabilities and career and to learn from the advice and experience of others without compromising yourself.

The Origins of This Book

This book originated almost twenty years ago when I chaired the first national conference on "The Outer Limits of Human Performance" for what is now the the federal government's Department of Education. Bud Hodgkinson, a visionary director of the National Institute of Education, sponsored the conference out of his organization's director's fund. He and I were both distressed at the myopic focus of national education and training efforts on basic skills, minimum standards, and entry-level job skills—all human minimums. Even with such low expectations, the national education establishment was having trouble reaching minimum levels, however they were defined. Bud and I thought that exploring ways of educating people to achieve very high levels of competence might break open this self-limiting focus and enable national education not only to reach minimum standards but to far surpass them as a matter of course.

Trained as a scientist and a researcher, I was sad to find remarkably little scientific data about high levels of human performance. There was a scientific literature on certain high-performing segments of society and culture—particularly athletes—and some on high-performing teams in a variety of fields. Enormous amounts of anecdotal evidence existed in the form of recipes from successful people about how they had made it. Yet there were almost no studies of individuals or teams who started out average and went through a process of becoming high performing. That is, we knew almost nothing about the learning process as it applied to most people. Even the studies that focused on high performers were limited. Athletic profiles tended to begin after an athlete had been selected for a team or an Olympic training camp. Training of famous artists seemed not to begin until after an exceptional performer had been accepted into a national ballet school, for instance. Military special forces or such elites as fighter pilots were extraordinarily selective—only the top few even made it into the programs. In each case, normal people were selected out. The training techniques that worked for highly developed candidates might or might not apply to the population at large.

I had become familiar with some of the extraordinarily powerful education and training techniques that had grown out of the group dynamics, group therapy, and human potential movements of the 1960s. These techniques were beneficial for people who found themselves and their lives trapped in closed loops that seemed to go nowhere and that gave them no satisfaction. The training techniques had the power to open these people up, to give them insight into what had trapped them, and to encourage them to take responsibility for their lives. Many came out of such programs ready and eager to get on with their lives.

Even so, such methodologies provided remarkably little guidance about what was right for an individual or about what to do with all that eager new energy. Therapists could help clients to identify what wasn't working for them. Support groups and other mechanisms could encourage people to do something different. Yet no one had anything particularly helpful for the person who wanted insight into what he or she actually should do. Particular techniques, such as assertiveness training, could be invaluable in specific situations. But those techniques all involved some implicit general concept, for instance, that one should simply be assertive if one wanted to remedy a problem. Assertiveness training did not empower people to be assertive in order to achieve a specific purpose, much less identify what that purpose might be. In the same way, therapists often worked with an implicit model of a fully developed personality, or an ideal marriage, which did not acknowledge that human development and human relationships take a huge variety of forms, many of which can be quite satisfying. I was skeptical of anything that did not honor human diversity.

So for nearly two years I explored how high levels of human performance actually happened. Unable to pursue this line of study in the federal government when administrations changed, I left and formed my own consulting company.

The Discovery of Individual High Performance Patterns

I began in 1980 by interviewing people in great depth about times when they had experienced doing something extraordinarily well. I taped the interviews and analyzed them all. Since the interviewees were all more or less ordinary people who had suddenly produced outstanding results, I suspected that a process was involved. I wanted to amass a body of descriptive data about that process and discover how it actually happened. I figured that such data would provide some real guidance for us all. I transcribed each interview, or summarized the person's process, and went on to another. I assumed that I would find some set of rules or principles that would be true for everyone.

I soon noticed that every one of the people whom I interviewed had had the experience of suddenly producing outstanding results of some kind. In other words, the experience of unexpectedly outstanding success was universal. I also found that most people dismissed the experience as luck, not as something that they could repeat. This gave me a clue as to why so little was known about it.

But my most extraordinary discovery was this: The process was different for everyone.

As I assembled case after case, I realized that each person had a consistent process that led to outstanding results. Yet no two people were the same. In fact, the variety was astonishing. Now, more than a decade later, having amassed thousands of cases—a formidable data base of how people actually produce their best work—I find that this conclusion is still true. I began to call this unique process a person's High Performance Pattern. That label stuck. A High Performance Pattern is a person's own individual success process.

It's not that there aren't various types of patterns. Of course there are. Any collection of thousands of examples of anything can be categorized. I am deeply indebted to Professor Robert Quinn, chair of the Organizational Behavior Department of the University of Michigan's School of Business Administration, and Gretchen Spreitzer, his top graduate student, now an assistant professor at the University of Southern California, for carrying out the first rigorous academic analysis of a large sample of High Performance Patterns. They identified

a number of types of patterns and compared the results with other typologies discussed in the management literature. Their results tended
to validate High Performance Patterns and to extend the existing management literature in a number of intriguing ways. The concluding
chapter of this book summarizes their findings.

What I found, however, and what serves as the basis for my work
of the last dozen years, is that the nuances unique to each pattern, not
its similarities to other patterns, are what actually make the difference
in an individual's performance. People are like other people when they
do ordinary, competent work. They become uniquely themselves
when they do their best work. I found early on that I could use High
Performance Patterns to work with people individually, comparing
how they were doing some critical activity with how they would have
done it if they had followed their own path to success. Invariably the
comparison turned up something they could do to be more on pattern. When they followed their own success process, they achieved
better, more sustainable results. This finding proved particularly valuable when their selected activity wasn't going well and they didn't
know what they were doing wrong. For some years, I made a decent
living consulting just with individuals while continuing to amass cases
for my research.

In retrospect, I am grateful that I was suddenly offered a chance to
present a seminar on what I was learning. Jim Kouzes, whose books
on leadership have since led to national fame, was then director of the
Executive Development Center at the Leavey School of Business and
Administration of the University of Santa Clara. He knew of my work
and offered me a chance to participate in a series of four offerings, in
the first of which Tom Peters talked about his new book, *In Search of
Excellence* (Peters and Waterman, 1982). Since that book dealt with
organizational high performance, Jim wanted me to follow up by
addressing the issue of individual high performance. I eagerly accepted.

Jim's former partner, Roger Harrison, a highly respected consultant, friend, and mentor in the early days, then made an invaluable
suggestion. He recommended that instead of presenting a seminar
about what I was learning, I should put people through the experience
of finding their own High Performance Patterns. The experience itself
would be the real teacher. I followed his advice. The seminar went

over very well—within a few months it had been picked up by Procter & Gamble, IBM, the Memorex Corporation, Wang Laboratories, and Digital Equipment Corporation. I found myself in the training business.

The overarching effort over the past decade has been to develop the technology of High Performance Patterns, learn how to use them, and train individuals and managers to use them in organizational settings to produce better, more sustainable, and more rewarding results. We have come a long way. We now know how to find a person's High Performance Pattern with a high degree of reliability and certainty. We can also train others to find it. We also have a well-developed rating system for maintaining quality control when lots of people are engaged in identifying and using patterns .

We have learned how to use individual High Performance Patterns in working with teams so that team members engage their individual success processes in carrying out their work. The results of team-building efforts that tapped team members' High Performance Patterns have been particularly gratifying. We are now engaged in developing management systems so that entire organizations can routinely manage people the way they work best by making use of their High Performance Patterns.

The Structure of This Book

This book is filled with examples. If I only talk about what we do, people can still be confused about how it is like or not like some other approach. However, if I show examples, most questions disappear, and people concentrate on the approach itself. In all the cases presented in these chapters, I am also an active participant. I describe how I worked with the individual in question to achieve the desired result, not as an ego boost to myself but rather to illustrate how the process of generating insight in order to improve a person's performance is usually a cooperative effort between the person and someone else. I have tried to show how to use a person's own High Performance Pattern when interacting with him or her, because I hope that others, particularly managers, can learn to do what I did.

While I encourage people to try to find their own High Performance Patterns, I also have tried to be honest about the difficulties. In answer to question 12 at the end of Part I, I deal with the advantages and problems of identifying one's own pattern.

The structure of the book is simple: The Introduction and Chapter 1 provide the context and define the key concepts used in the book. Then, Part I describes how we discover a person's High Performance Pattern and answers a number of questions about the validity of patterns. Part II contains individual case studies demonstrating how High Performance Patterns can be applied. Each case study shows how High Performance Patterns helped to resolve a specific problem or maximize an opportunity. Part III presents case studies involving pairs of people who used High Performance Patterns to develop more effective working relationships.

Each Part has an introductory section and a concluding chapter with answers to typical questions. The book's Conclusion follows the three Parts.

All the examples in this book relate the experiences of real people taken from our data base. Of course, the names, locations, and corporate affiliations—and on occasion the sex—have been changed to protect the privacy of those involved.

You do not need to read the case examples in order. If you feel like you are getting the idea, pick only the examples that interest you or perhaps those about people who face problems similar to your own.

Acknowledgments

The process of developing a new technology, such as the one described in this book, owes a great deal to individuals in organizations who spotted the power of the idea and were willing to bring the process and related programs into their companies. Our method could never be what it is today if it had not been championed by many people. In addition to those whom I have already mentioned, I would like to thank my immediate boss in Washington, D.C., Philip Austin, who allowed me to focus on high performance; Fred Kanter, who helped me find the first set of clients on whom I tested the methodology; and Rich Silton, who first used the technology at Memorex and who later, with his partner Phil Bookman, has supported me for many years. A number of people helped to institutionalize this methodology at IBM; thanks to Richie Herink, who first brought me into the company; David Allen, who personally convinced managers to use the program; John Florkowski and Ed Rosenberg, who along with David became a team of champions for the program; and Dick Butler and Frank Skidmore, who used the program with all their managers in significant segments of the company.

I am grateful to Ron Gibson, now of Digital Equipment Corporation, who first brought me into Wang Laboratories; Virginia Reck, who championed the program at Wang and who, for many years as a senior consultant in the CSC/Index consulting company, has opened doors for me to new clients; Don Arnoudse and Phil Lawrence of CSC/Index, who arranged for testing internally and with Index clients, respectively; Joanne Small, who first brought me into Digital; Bob Hoyt and Judy Gustafson of Digital, who selected our program as the core methodology for a special training of the Digital sales force; Nancy Uridil of Procter & Gamble, who first brought the program into a plant, and Terry Cole, who managed that plant; Bob DeSisto, who first brought the program to Pioneer Hi-Bred International and later to Scott Paper; Karen Johnsen and Lisa Mullan of Pioneer Hi-Bred who became the first internal corporate trainers certified in the methodology; Don Powers of Control Data; Cookie Pettee of the East Bay Municipal Utilities District; Bert Hughes of Pacific Bell; Erica Ross-Krieger of Pacific Gas and Electric; Jim Snyder, who first brought the program to Pfizer Pharmaceuticals, Grant Denison, who picked it up there and brought me into Searle Pharmaceuticals and later Monsanto; Bob Whitehead and Eduardo Rabello, who used the approach extensively with their people at Searle; Jim Baldes of Weyerhaeuser; Bob Potter, president of the Chemical Group of Monsanto, where I have been working for nearly two years with the management board, and three of his vice presidents, Dave Sliney, Charlie Ross, and John Ferguson; and Victoria Franchetti Haynes, who headed one of the Chemical Group's R&D centers and used the approach to reorganize how the center conducted its work.

I would also like to thank Ed Hinkelman and Kelle Olwyler, who early on cast their lot with me and this technology, who have been invaluable in developing it, and who over the last year have taken on more work so that I could be free to write this book; members of our training and consulting staff, particularly Geri Blitzman, Dee Thompson, Richard Snyder, Terry Pearce, and in the early days, Marsha Ostrer, who have freely added their ideas to the development of our programs and processes; Merry Selk, who helped me write the first draft; Chansonette Wedemeyer, who edited the final version; Al Alschuler and Peter Stroh, who took time from their busy schedules to critique the manuscript; and finally my wife, Kathleen, who seems to have understood from the beginning, sometimes better than I did, that developing this methodology was really a life's calling for me and who supported me through the ups and downs of making it a reality.

San Anselmo, California   Jerry L. Fletcher
June 1993

INTRODUCTION

Individual Uniqueness
and Real-World Complexity

As an experienced manager or executive or simply as someone with significant life experience, you know that abstract solutions are of limited use in complex situations. Although an attractive theory sometimes works well in a real situation, the reality that you encounter is usually more messy. Even with an idea that you know is sound in the abstract, you struggle to find a workable application or variation that will give you better results than the ones you get following your customary procedures.

A common dilemma illustrates this principle. Let's say your boss has unintentionally been making unrealistic and unreasonable demands of you. His expectations set you up for failure, which neither of you really wants. You know that you need to be more assertive with him. It is in your best interests, and in his, that you negotiate limits and set priorities for the tasks that he has assigned.

"So," you say to yourself swallowing hard, "be assertive." You have read all the books on assertiveness. You have been through assertiveness training. You know the concept thoroughly in the abstract. But now *you* have to confront *your* boss. Obviously, you want positive results. You also know that he is under a lot of pressure. This is a tough time in your business. He may become testy if you appear to be wanting to shirk your tasks.

If you are lucky, some assertiveness technique that you have learned will fit your situation perfectly. Even so, there is a large unknown. How exactly should you employ an assertiveness technique with your boss in this specific situation? What if he responds in an unexpected way? How will you put the technique into effective action? Do you trust yourself and the technique? Do you have the courage to try it out?

High Performance Patterns

The chapters that follow introduce you to an innovative, profoundly practical tool—the individual High Performance Pattern—that enables you to make any idea or technique your own and to use it with the kind of personal integrity that gives you confidence in such messy situations as the one just sketched. You will also learn how to use the tool by seeing how it is applied in a large number of diverse cases.

This tool and the associated techniques of application have been worked out over the last decade by myself and my associates at High Performance Dynamics in work with great numbers of individuals and organizations. When I use the word *we* in this book, I mean myself and my professional consultants at HPD. When I use the word *I*, it is either because I was the consultant involved or because it emphasizes the dialogue nature of the process.

Defining High Performance

We define high performance as producing results much better than expected both in individuals and in organizations. This book describes techniques for consistently finding much better courses of action in messy (that is, real) situations, and it shows how to carry out these actions effectively. The process of managing yourself or others allows you to find and implement ways of correcting problems systematically. It enables you to identify and exploit high-performance opportunities, that is, situations that have the potential for producing better than expected results.

The High Performance Pattern is a precise description of the unique sequence of steps that an individual consistently follows when he or she carries out an activity that has highly successful results.

Knowing your own and your employees' High Performance Patterns will greatly simplify and shorten your struggle to find much better courses of action. A High Performance Pattern can be used in any relationship and any situation, business or personal. It is a truly unique, flexible, and effective problem-solving tool.

Discovering your High Performance Pattern frees you from the apparent conflict between doing a task your unique way and complying with your organization's prescribed or expected methods. High Performance Patterns are designed to enable a manager and an employee, working within the constraints of organizational policy, to come up with a performance solution that is mutually acceptable to both. In this way, the employee can accomplish tasks in the way best suited to his or her own success process while still complying with organizational requirements. As the case studies in subsequent chapters show, once a person's High Performance Pattern has been identified, it can be used as a guide both for correcting current problems and for planning future action. When used properly, High Performance Patterns engender true win-win outcomes.

Throughout the rest of the book I will elaborate on how people and organizations actually achieve high performance. The case studies of successful people who have achieved their very best by applying their High Performance Patterns will show what it takes to get to a high-performance mode and how to sustain it. Keep in mind that each case study you read is the story of an actual person, in an actual, messy, complicated real-life situation. These case studies will show you how managers and employees, consultants and clients, friends, and even mothers and daughters have used High Performance Patterns to focus and direct their search for a mutually acceptable solution to a difficult problem.

Characteristics of Effective Managers

The fundamental task of management is to deploy people well. Over time, a manager assigns available personnel to an array of important tasks, motivates them during the time it takes to complete the work, and then redeploys them to new activities. The way in which a manager accomplishes these operations determines his or her degree of effectiveness. Effective managers accurately match individual talents with necessary tasks. They motivate individual employees by finding the particular challenges, rewards, types of support, and amounts of freedom that bring out the best in each of them. And they redeploy their people at the right time to maintain and improve the organization's momentum.

In contrast, ineffective managers often mismatch people with tasks. Because they do not discern what motivates each individual to sustain successful and efficient job performance, their employees waste valuable time and resources in unmotivated behaviors. Under such managers, people tend to languish on assignments long after making their maximum contributions. Meanwhile, other crucial activities to which they could have been assigned flounder for lack of personnel and resources.

In view of the crucial nature of deploying, motivating, and redeploying people, the standard tools for equipping a manager to perform this function well are woefully inadequate. Methods for deploying, motivating, tracking, and redeploying people remain primitive when compared with other process-improvement technologies. Although knowledge and skills inventories, measures of character traits, categorizations of personality types, and typologies of management styles can be helpful, they are ultimately very limited in their ability to guide managers or employees. They give little insight into how to get the best work from a unique individual assigned to a particular task in a complex real-life situation.

Managers want practical help. When your employee has a problem on a project, you as manager may need to make a fast, accurate diagnosis and find a powerful way of getting the individual back on track. Specific insights regarding what the person might do to correct the problem will help you do that far more effectively than general characteristics describing some abstract category of people into which your employee fits. When you assign an employee to a new activity, both you and the employee need specific information to ascertain the best approach to the task. And when your organization adds a person whom you don't know to your team, you need an insightful and affirming way to assess what he or she can do and what you can count on.

Managers are also keenly interested in motivating their people. As manager, you have two primary goals: to get your employees productively engaged in their work in a sustained way and to avoid making costly deployment mistakes. Wouldn't you jump at the chance to have a tool that would help you know how and when to move an employee to a different assignment? Wouldn't you love to keep your employees challenged? Wouldn't you welcome a practical method that enabled you to sustain your employees' motivation and output?

The catch-22 in management training is that, although general guidelines may be helpful for novice managers, experienced managers know that they must usually rely on gut judgments when it comes to actual management decisions. Even advice from senior managers is often of little use. And although managerial instinct grows more accurate and insightful as experience accrues, most managers would appreciate something more definitive for their decision-making processes.

As this book proceeds and I unfold the way in which High Performance Patterns work, you will see that they provide the decision-making tool that you need. High Performance Patterns and the process of using them directly address what managers really need to know in order to deploy, motivate, and redeploy their people—and themselves—effectively.

New Organizational Realities

It is hard enough to do an outstanding job of management even in relatively stable working conditions. But current competitive pressures have spawned massive changes in the business arena worldwide. These changes complicate the manager's deployment job astronomically. Companies are finding it increasingly necessary to break up and recombine existing arrangements of people. These recombinations often throw unacquainted people together and give them unfamiliar goals and objectives, with unsettling rapidity. Ubiquitous corporate downsizings make a manager's capacity for effective action in the face of great uncertainty and rapid change increasingly critical.

As organizations become increasingly flatter, fifteen direct reports are commonplace, and twenty-five are far from unknown. The traditional span-of-control organizational principles no longer make sense. As a manager in today's business climate, you don't need a means of personnel control. You need an alternative approach, one that inspires your employees and gives them the confidence and courage to do their jobs successfully. Your people need to know that they can seize opportunities and make successes out of a fluid organizational environment.

A Practical Process for Mutual Engagement

What does such an alternative approach to managing people look like? In the model presented in this book, each manager and each employee has a personal, individual guide identifying his or her best way of working. With these guides in hand, you and the individual employee identify which assignments are best, what rewards and support will motivate the best possible contribution, and how you will both know when the employee will be more productive if he or she moves on to another assignment. Manager and employee collaborate to determine the work plan.

Because you devise the plan jointly and because it is based on you and your employee's best ways of working, you eliminate the need for most controlling supervision. Motivation and the accurate match of talent with task are integral to the process of determining the assignment. The fact that controlling supervision is not needed frees the manager up for more value-added tasks. You both can trust that your plan will work, even in the face of great uncertainty. Moreover, the flexibility innate in this planning method facilitates its application to a wide range of tasks and problem situations.

Our High Performance Patterns have helped organizations all over the world to find useful solutions to the challenges posed by tasks and personnel. When you have identified the High Performance Patterns of your employees and you use them properly, they facilitate specific discussion of each person's strengths as well as his or her needs for support and rewards. These discussions make it possible to tailor an individual plan for each assignment that will empower your employee for outstanding achievement. By using High Performance Patterns, your employee wins, your organization wins, and you win.

Even with positive techniques producing alignment and vision, the effective manager needs tools defining proactive, aggressive actions that can turn vision into reality. High Performance Patterns and the process of using them are such a tool. And because patterns describe the actual process by which someone succeeds in the real world, they empower employees to do their best without running the risk of irresponsible or destructive behaviors. By their very nature, patterns preclude mistakes made out of ignorance or lack of experience.

Distinctive Features

While many of the features of High Performance Patterns will become clear as you progress through the book, there are advantages to my telling you early on what is coming. In the chapters and case studies that follow, you will see that High Performance Patterns have a number of distinct advantages over other tools available to the manager.

- They are written in natural language. High Performance Patterns use the employee's own words. No expert has to interpret statistical printouts. They facilitate informed discussion between manager and employee (and between peers) to determine how each individual should be deployed, what specific rewards and support are needed for effective work, and when it is time to move on to another task.

- They produce fast results. Since a High Performance Pattern is a scrupulously detailed, step-by-step description of the person's best working process, finding where someone is off pattern when a task or activity flounders is easy. Both manager and employee can focus quickly and accurately on what needs to change for improvement.

- They produce nondisruptive solutions. By definition, a person's High Performance Pattern has worked repeatedly in his or her life. It is naturally and fundamentally nondisruptive. Not that some steps along the path are not disruptive: anyone who consistently produces results has to shake up a process that isn't working. But when the shake-up methods work consistently, the disruption is fine-tuned and appropriate.

- They apply to a broad range of situations. High Performance Patterns are the individually consistent ways that people have of being effective in the world. As such, they are derived from, and apply to, such diverse circumstances as solving a technical problem (What's your way of investigating a problem and figuring out what to do?), resolving an interpersonal difficulty (What's your way of doing this? What's mine? Where are we in conflict? How can we control or eliminate the conflict?), planning how to do something (What's your way of getting something done effectively? How can you do this present task accordingly?), and figuring out what's wrong when something isn't going well (What would I be doing if I were on pattern? Where am I off?).

- They give people confidence. High Performance Patterns have the greatest appeal for mature, experienced, and successful people on the lookout for the latest cutting-edge technology. These seasoned achievers already have the confidence to act, and once they know precisely how they succeed, they just succeed some more. For less-experienced people, patterns provide the confidence that they need in order to act effectively in the face of uncertainty. Over the years, we have developed effective, simple-to-use formats for presenting the insights of High Performance Patterns, and we have become increasingly effective at enabling people to use their patterns.

  Lines of action derived from a person's High Performance Pattern instill an inherent confidence. You know it will work—the solution fits you like a glove. Your manager knows it will work—even with unusual elements, he or she can see in the specifics of your pattern why it will be effective. For seasoned achievers and the less experienced alike, patterns remove the common discrepancy between knowing what to do and having the confidence to do it.

- They help strangers get to know each other. New employees and their managers must get to know each other fast. For the manager, accurate deployment and for employees, high performance depend on accurate, mutual under-standing. Since High Performance Patterns promote discussion, the sharing of experiences between employee and manager can focus directly on the specifics of an assignment and on the forms of support and reward that will bring the new person up to speed quickly.

- They honor differences. Learning to use individual High Performance Patterns, whether your own or those of the people whom you manage, promotes profound respect for individual differences. Through patterns, you come to understand the differences that actually make a difference in how effective a person is in the world. These are the differences that we need to respect and honor.

Many American companies are now deeply involved in some form of diversity training that addresses the ways in which sexual, racial, and cultural stereotypes unconsciously limit the contributions of large segments of the work force. These issues are important both in general and for an organization's peak effectiveness. In order to overcome sexual, racial, and cultural barriers, people must first become aware of them. However, once we have made the decision to confront and surmount these barriers, we still have to deal with individual differences. Optimizing an individual's contribution still has paramount importance. High Performance Patterns pinpoint, like no other process, exactly the actions that produce the best results for each person. Training in High Performance Patterns is thus an appropriate sequel to corporate diversity training.

After this overview, let us turn now to the concrete characteristics of the High Performance Pattern tool.

1

A Practical Definition
of High Performance

For more than ten years, we have identified the High Performance Patterns of more than five thousand people. We have worked with corporate executives, entrepreneurs, small business managers, and working people from all over the world. Ours is the only existing large data base containing detailed descriptions of the ways in which people produce their best results.

This information reveals two distinct ways in which people get results. We call them *grind-it-out mode* and *high-performance mode*.

As Figure 1 shows, in grind-it-out mode, people have predetermined definitions of the results they are to achieve, and they strive for those results. As the name suggests, the process is hard and grinding, and once the result has been achieved, most people simply feel exhausted and relieved. Meeting a deadline or making a quota are common examples.

High-performance mode contrasts sharply with this picture. When people recount a high-performance experience, there was a point at which the activity took off and seemed to have a life of its own. The people involved began to delight in the unexpectedly good results that they were achieving. The experience had the quality of being easy and flowing, even if participants were tired at the end. And, in contrast to a grind-it-out experience, people at the end of a high-

11

performance experience are wistful. They wish it could have continued, and in some sense they fear that they'll never be able to have it happen again.

Any person who has attained even a modest level of success has the capacity to grind out almost any task at an acceptable level of performance, even under difficult circumstances. We can all discipline ourselves, drive ourselves, and pull all-nighters to meet deadlines if we have to. However, very few people actually do their best work in this way. And this mode of working has significant consequences: exhaustion and burnout. No one can operate in grind-it-out mode for long without a serious drop in performance. It simply is not a sustainable route to high performance.

Figure 1. Two Ways of Getting Results

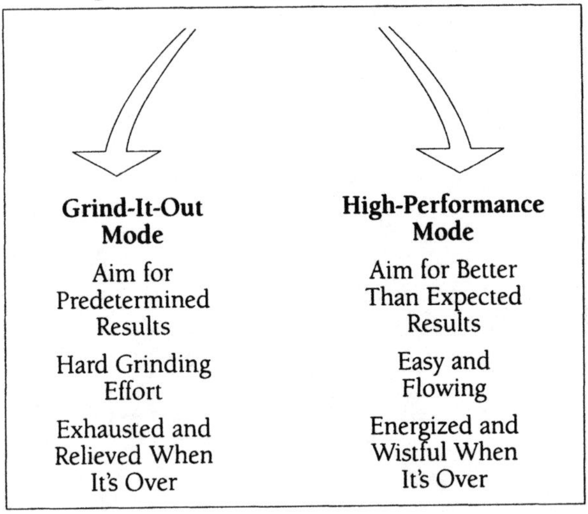

Grind-It-Out Mode	High-Performance Mode
Aim for Predetermined Results	Aim for Better Than Expected Results
Hard Grinding Effort	Easy and Flowing
Exhausted and Relieved When It's Over	Energized and Wistful When It's Over

Despite this seemingly obvious fact, many companies unwittingly keep employees in grind-it-out mode as a matter of policy. They use various pressures and incentives to enforce conformity to company-sanctioned methods, believing that this is either the best or the only way to sustain results over time. The number of companies that drive their people through a combination of tight deadlines, peer pressure, management sanctions, and rewards for winning is staggering. The consequences of these policies are often highly visible: Personnel are exhausted and burned out.

Not only is the use of external pressures and incentives to meet goals and deadlines personally detrimental to employees, it produces the kind of organizational peak-performance curve illustrated in Figure 2. Employees expend enormous effort to produce the required result. As soon as the goal is reached, output drops off precipitously. Productivity remains at an ebb until the next deadline approaches, which once again spurs personnel to frantic and exhausting action.

Figure 2. Peak-Performance Curve

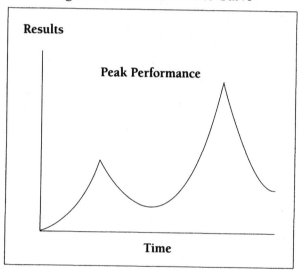

Anyone in sales knows this graph. The peaks correspond to monthly or quarterly closings. Most managers in other businesses can also identify with this picture. That's because most organizations function this way. And this periodic peaking is the classic result of keeping people in grind-it-out mode.

In contrast, high-performance mode generates outstanding results and enables an organization to achieve much higher, more sustainable performance with less effort and less stress. It involves helping people find a way to do their work that is consistent with their High Performance Patterns, their best ways of working. Using their patterns elevates their performance to a new level. They can sustain performance at this new level because the means are integral to the person who has reached it. As Figure 3 indicates, the graph that results from managing people according to the principles of high-performance mode shows individuals reaching and consolidating new levels of performance.

Figure 3. Sustained High Performance

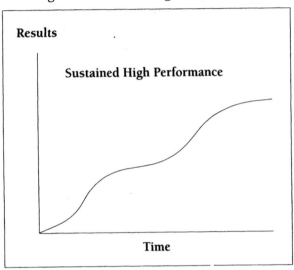

We have used High Performance Patterns to improve performance in real-world situations for more than ten years by helping people find the way of achieving results that matches their personal success pattern. You will see as you read on that, by using High Performance Patterns to adjust their actions deliberately, individuals and companies have achieved payoffs that far outweigh the effort required to identify the pattern. Results often improve by 25 to 50 percent. And most of the time the new level can be sustained naturally. Because of our experience with helping individuals and organizations achieve high performance, we firmly believe that grind-it-out mode should be regarded at best as the fallback position. Companies should use it only as the very last resort.

Experiencing High Performance

When we begin to discover an individual's High Performance Pattern, we start by asking the person to recall times when something that he or she did worked better than expected. We particularly look for situations that seemed to take on a life of their own and blossomed into achievements that astonished everyone. Every person has had this kind of experience at some time. Some of our clients tell of modest situations when everything went unexpectedly well. Others relate complex situations that they were able to resolve without overwhelming effort. The following examples from our files illustrate the variety of scenarios that we have encountered:

- A salesman remembered a particular time when he walked into a meeting with a tough client expecting a modest sale at best. He emerged with the largest sale he had ever made and with a promise for future orders.

- A manager recalled a time when, as a recent college graduate with a broadcasting degree but no experience, she wanted a job so badly that she called the vice president of a major network in New York. She managed to get through to him. She arranged a job interview for a significant position and won her first job over much more experienced competition.

- A public relations specialist told about a time when he was a volunteer in a small nonprofit organization. The governor of his state had vetoed a bill that was important to the work of his organization. Although our client had no previous political experience, he got so angry that he organized a two-week grassroots campaign that led to the overturning of the governor's veto. Much to the young man's surprise, the governor hired him as a public relations staff member for his next campaign.

Anyone who thinks about it long enough can identify such high-performance experiences in his or her own life, experiences that produced results far exceeding those anticipated. We do not define high performance experiences as those that produce world-class results. Although world-class results may be an occasional outcome, to define high performance in such a way would place the experience beyond the reach of all but the gifted few. We might harbor the personal illusion that we could do world-class work if we wanted to, but for most of us that is an unattainable dream. Moreover, holding out for world-class performance can actually cripple us, keeping us from achieving our actual best with our own unique abilities and limitations. High-performance experiences occur within the realm of the personally plausible and as such are truly empowering.

As I will explain later, not only do studies of world-class performers have very little to tell us about how ordinary people produce unexpectedly good results, the very fact that we think they have something to teach is often debilitating. For instance, most of the techniques promoted in popular books and magazines are peak-performance techniques. By definition, peak-performance techniques are not sustainable. Even the people who promote these methods cannot sustain them. They use them to peak for a particular athletic meet, a particular performance, or a particular event. The popular press does not describe the whole process, as we do in identifying High Performance Patterns. Without a detailed explanation, the reader cannot possibly understand the incredibly disciplined, sustained practice and preparation needed to create the foundation that allows the peaking techniques to work. And without such a foundation, most peak-performance techniques are of limited use.

Unlike popularized peak-performance techniques, our definition of high performance is relevant for all people, regardless of educational level, experience, age, gender, ethnicity, or opportunity. It draws on each individual's unique experience of high performance, so that he or she can consciously repeat the process in other situations. Any company that equips its employees to produce their own better than expected results will see across-the-board improvements. And these improvements will far surpass the results of a few miracle workers. If a company implements our processes so that a thousand people do 5 percent better every quarter, no matter what their jobs are, it has the real strategy for producing a high-performance organization. This book will show you how to make that happen.

Each Person Has a Unique High Performance Pattern

Each individual has only one High Performance Pattern. Regardless of the nature or context of the activity in which the individual is engaged, he or she follows a consistent and unique sequence of specific actions when achieving his or her personal best. Each person's pattern is as unique as a fingerprint. Since it is so consistent, once the individual's pattern has been identified, it is a highly effective guide to future action. It maps out how the person can produce outstanding work consistently .

How can you use the pattern embedded in your high-performance experiences to improve your future chances for success? The most effective way of maximizing results is to employ the pattern of behavior that already works. This means that if you are true to the success process that already works for you, you will produce much faster, more effective, and more sustainable improvements than you can by imitating others you think are better or by adopting unfamiliar new ways of working that may not fit you at all.

People Can Be Managed to Produce Outstanding Results

Our finding that each person has a consistent and unique way of being successful supports our radical attitude: People will produce better results if they are allowed, supported, and encouraged to work in the way that they work best.

Each individual can learn how he or she works best. Each individual can find ways to do assigned tasks that are consistent with his or her best ways of working. By the same process, a manager can learn how each person on the team works best and can then assign work and provide support to keep employees true to their individual ways of producing the best results.

Universal Motivators Can't Do the Job

Most efforts to enhance organizational productivity look for universal motivators that can generate more motivated workers. These universal motivators range from heightened manager-employee communication and mutual involvement in decision making to bonuses, salary incentives, work redesign, and competitions.

Since our data base contains accurate descriptions of how people actually produce their best work, we can test any potential universal motivator against what actually motivates individuals. Analyses of a sample of High Performance Patterns show a vast variety of unique factors critical to the success of individual people. When we look at the entire sequence of actions that a person performs when he or she takes an activity from beginning to end and produces better than expected results, the extent and degree of the individual differences that we find are staggering. No one motivator will work for more than a small portion of the whole process and for a small percentage of people.

Thus, we can demonstrate that any universal motivator in fact isn't a universal factor at all. Any one motivational technique will fit certain people, and it will be effective for those whom it fits. But for every person that the technique fits, it will neither fit nor motivate the great majority. And there will always be those individuals that the technique will discourage or even disable.

A cursory look at the use of competition and contests as sales motivators makes this point very clear. Some people have High Performance Patterns that are very competitive. These individuals respond well to contests, and they often work harder during such events. They love to win, and often they do. Others are motivated by entirely different factors. Some salespeople are motivated by serving clients truly well. People who have this motivation in their pattern will not sell a client something inappropriate to the client's need, even if losing a sale means they will not make their quarterly quota. Others are motivated by finding the very best solution to some problem, and to the degree that a contest pressures them to sell quick-and-dirty solutions just to beat someone else, they will actively resist.

Analyses of our data base show that as motivational factors, competition and contests fit the High Performance Patterns of only a few. Many of our conversations with sales managers have confirmed this finding. In their experience, contests truly motivate only about 20 percent of their salespeople. The other 80 percent go through the motions. Typically, the winner of a sales contest is one in a handful of employees. The others do not even try to compete.

I will elaborate on and clarify this point later in the book. For now, just keep in mind that each person has his or her own unique pattern. Only the motivators that fit and reinforce that pattern are effective. It is true that external motivating factors, such as involvement in decision making, tight deadlines, or incentive bonuses, do fit some people's High Performance Patterns and thus motivate them. At the same time, these external motivators miss the principal factors that drive most other people toward excellence. For that majority, these particular external universal motivators have no particular effect. If you really want to motivate your employee, you must know and use his or her High Performance Pattern.

Using High Performance Patterns

Go with What Already Works

A few pages back, I noted that for most people the key to success is to identify what already works for them and to go with that. The example of executive Warren Marks illustrates what we mean by going with what already works. How I got Warren and his staff to work with rather than fight his best way of working will show you how we apply our principles in an actual situation. This is what I found when I began to work with Warren:

When he first sought to understand and use his High Performance Pattern to improve his performance, Warren Marks was thirty-five and already considered a great success within his profession and his company, the Biocenter Group. As vice president of planning and business development, Warren was invited to give major addresses at biotechnology meetings throughout the United States, Canada, and Europe. His presentations were always brilliant. He always tailored them to his audiences in a way that bordered on genius. Warren seemed able to sense what an audience wanted. He always gave his listeners a visionary perspective on their goals, and he always seemed to have up-to-the-minute data and information.

In spite of his success, Warren Marks considered himself a procrastinator. His staff concurred. He always seemed to wait until the last minute to prepare a presentation, and sometimes he was still making changes the night before the event. He and his staff regarded this habit as a significant shortcoming. Despite the considerable efforts of his staff to get Warren to complete his speeches a few days early so they could prepare the slides and data analyses for his presentation, the day and the night immediately before a speech always saw a frenzy of activity.

Even when his staff succeeded in getting him to write an early draft, Warren always ended up rewriting it at the last minute. Everything else in his department screeched to a halt while his staff revised data analyses and reworked slides for the rewritten speech. Yet time after time, the presentation itself was as smooth as silk. Warren gave a truly elegant speech and answered questions deftly. A well-deserved ovation followed.

In spite of his success, Warren worried about the burden that he put on his staff. He wanted to overcome his procrastination. He hoped that finding his High Performance Pattern would help him do that. He believed that his work would improve if he stopped procrastinating.

When I use Warren's case as an example in a training session, I stop at this point and ask people to imagine that they are Warren's friend or a consultant working with Warren's team. What would they recommend? How would they proceed? Many people, even experienced consultants, jump in quickly to make recommendations. They bring up personal examples of their own procrastination. They describe how they overcame the habit. Sometimes they share anecdotes about other people who have struggled with the problem.

Stop and Get the Pattern First

Our approach differs radically from that of most other consulting techniques. Before we get involved at all in thinking about solutions, we stop to spend some time finding out how the client works when he is most successful. Once we find his High Performance Pattern, we compare what he is doing in the actual situation with what he would be doing if he were on pattern—that is, if he were dealing with the problem in the way that works best for him.

Once we know the person's High Performance Pattern, we can address his or her problem by looking particularly for places where he or she has deviated from what works best. When we have identified the deviation, we try to find the simplest, most direct way of reintegrating the person with his or her own way of being successful. The solution often turns out to be a very simple action. And the person feels confident to take the corrective action because it fits. This process almost always produces significant results, because it does not involve trying to get the client to change.

So, to help Warren with his problem, we began by helping him to identify the pattern responsible for his success. I established Warren's High Performance Pattern by analyzing experiences in which he had produced unexpectedly good results. Through this process, we discovered that what appeared to be procrastination in Warren's behavior really wasn't, at least as generally understood. This insight helped Warren and his staff see how to work together more effectively. Instead of forcing Warren to try to change this procrastination pattern, both he and his staff learned to take advantage of it, to cooperate with it.

Find High Performance Patterns in Detailed Stories

I began as we always do, by listening to and examining stories that Warren told about important high-performance experiences in his life—times when he produced results that were far better than he had expected. Warren was typical of our clients in that he recounted these stories with great enthusiasm and energy. Each story provided clues about the action steps that Warren had used to produce remarkable work. As Warren and I proceeded with the analysis, we assembled these clues into a complete pattern.

What distinguishes our consulting approach from others is that we do not look at the content of our clients' experiences or at common themes or surface similarities between them. Rather, we look under the surface for the process that our client used to be successful, at the pattern of actions in which he or she engaged. We look for answers to the question, What did this person do that produced the outstanding results? Warren's high-performance stories show how we get these answers.

Exploring Warren Marks's Experience

Warren told me about his first job interview and how it led to his first job and ultimately to his rapid rise to very early success in the biotechnology industry:

At the end of my first year at the Harvard Business School, one of the first companies holding interviews on campus was a major biotechnology company. I knew as sure as God made chickens that I had to have a practice interview somewhere. I had no intention of joining the biotechnology industry. I did the interview only as a warm-up exercise. I was the least prepared interviewee in the history of mankind. But it went well, and I must have managed to say what he wanted to hear.

I was offered a job as a summer intern, and took it. After I got my degree, I returned to the company as a full-time financial analyst. Early on, I was handed the job of figuring out how to take maximum advantage of the special investment tax incentives that had just been put into place for Puerto Rico. We already had substantial investments there, and it seemed like we had much to gain. I figured out what I thought was best and presented it to a major meeting of all the financial executives in the company. I only discovered afterward that my recommendation was the opposite of what the corporate CFO had recommended. It turned out that I was right and that he had missed a huge opportunity. After my first year, I was made assistant to the president.

On the surface, Warren Marks's success seems serendipitous: A warm-up exercise lands a job, and a surprising presentation launches a meteoric career. Outstanding performances often seem at first to be so unique and lucky as to be meaningless. But a successful performance is more than luck. In case after case, we have found that the seeming chance nature of success masks a person's consistent underlying process. Warren follows this process when he does his best work. And when the process is carefully described in writing, it can be become a detailed and practical guide for action unique to Warren.

I had Warren tell a number of other stories. He told me how, even before going to college, he had parlayed a childhood interest in raising flowers into a major business supplying cut flowers to restaurants and florists and how he had then sold the business for a considerable sum. He described some work that he had done through a church-sponsored summer program and how he had been led out of the area by a black gang leader when the riots broke out in the summer of 1967. All the stories that Warren told me of events in his life that had gone unexpectedly well had his High Performance Pattern as an underlying process. Here is what we found about Warren's best way of working.

Putting Ideas Together While Procrastinating

Every one of Warren's high-performance stories involved the appearance of being unprepared and of procrastinating. Warren seemed to wait until the last minute to do something critical, exactly as he waited to write his brilliant speeches. Yet when we analyzed all his stories, we found that Warren had in fact been very busy putting his ideas together during those times of apparent procrastination. He had been calling people, inquiring about the questions and concerns of his "audience," and trying out different ideas in his mind. In fact, when we looked at the story of his first job interview more closely, we found that Warren had done a lot of preparation for job interviews before showing up for the one that launched his career. He just hadn't expected to find a fit in the biotechnology industry, so he had regarded that particular interview as practice. What he had discovered, of course, was that he really knew how to accommodate the desires of his "audience."

Waiting Until Things Are Refined

In all his examples, waiting until the last moment enabled Warren to have everything fully refined and finely tailored before he went into overt action. Then when he finally acted, he was superb. Warren actually did his best work by waiting as long as possible—to the very last moment—before settling on what he was going to do. That was how he made sure that his line of action was the most precise and up-to-date.

As we plumbed his stories for insights into what Warren did when he was successful, we found that in every one of Warren's success stories

- he had been asked to deal with a situation in which resources were not being fully exploited (in the interview,

how he would handle certain difficult situations; in the
Puerto Rico case, how he would he maximize the tax benefits).

- he put together a "proactive, visionary strategy" based on
  a good sense of the "forces out there" (he captivated the
  interviewer with his imaginative method of solving the
  problem that he was given; his way of dealing with the tax
  incentives to invest in Puerto Rico was much more aggressive and visionary than that recommended by the vice
  president of finance.

- he tested and refined his strategy behind the scenes until
  he informally won acceptance from the audience (he had
  practiced handling tough interview questions with his
  roommates and friends; he tried out his Puerto Rico strategy on a number of key players who were going to be at
  the meeting).

- he presented his case with such class and attention to
  detail that everything else appeared second-rate by comparison (he was stunning in the interview; he presented
  an approach to the Puerto Rico situation that directly contradicted that proposed by the CFO and won the day).

Resolving the Problem with Warren's Speeches

Once we both knew Warren's High Performance Pattern, it became
clear that Warren was not procrastinating when he waited until the
last minute. He was preparing his speeches according to his own best
way of working. He waited until his grasp of the issues that concerned
his audience was total so that he could address them with scrupulous
attention to detail.

Once Warren's staff recognized his pattern, they acknowledged
that it worked, and work very well. If he wrote his speeches early,
Warren would feel compelled to change what he had written as new
information became available. His staff realized that, if they really
wanted to support his best work, they had to stop trying to make him
write his speeches early. They had to cooperate with his process.

But Warren's process caused his staff hardship. The staff decided that they could reduce their difficulties by planning their own work around Warren's High Performance Pattern. Since everyone agreed that all Warren's speeches were excellent, they began to consider how they could support him in working that way. Warren's staff acknowledged that it was exciting and fun to help prepare for his speeches, but they needed some time off afterward to recover from their extra efforts. They also needed advance notice of upcoming speeches so that they could clear their own calendars for Warren's last-minute rush. With these two changes, Warren's team found it quite easy to support his best work pattern.

Seeing the Positives in the Apparently Negative

Warren's case illustrates the difficulty of getting a person to see the positive in something that appears to be negative. Without the help of his pattern, Warren and his staff certainly did not see his seeming procrastination as an asset. But what to Warren's team looked like lack of organization and insensitivity was actually Warren's way of making sure that his speeches were exquisitely tailored to his audience.

We have found that no matter how bizarre an action may seem, if it shows up consistently in every one of a person's high-performance experiences, it has some positive function. We focus our effort on finding and supporting that function rather than on advocating a change in behavior. Time after time, as we find the ways a person works best, we also identify how he or she can be true both to his or her own patterns of high performance and to the organization's legitimate constraints. Going with what already works produces much better results.

Avoiding Comparisons to Idealized Models

People commonly think they know what they do to be successful, but they often are wrong. Few of us fully understand or respect the unique aspects of our personal ways of succeeding. We judge our own idiosyncratic behavior as bad, basing our judgment on the opinions of others. If it does not conform to what seems to be a more logically efficient mode of operating or one that a popular personality is promoting, we assume that it must be a detriment. For instance, you may compare your performance with some idealized concept of the perfect manager, or the perfect sales call, and find yourself wanting without ever determining whether the so-called perfect method is effective for you.

Warren and his staff judged the way he prepared speeches negatively by assuming that he should complete a speech days ahead of delivery so the staff could work normally to produce the slides and analyses. Warren could have forced himself to conform to this model. But if Warren had conformed, he would have produced "normal" to poor speeches. He would be operating in his own version of grind-it-out mode. His merely adequate speeches would be nowhere near the showstoppers that he was capable of. By discerning how he worked best and by playing to it, Warren not only rid himself of guilt and negative self-judgment, he kept his speeches top-notch.

Corporations often have rigid models for the right way of doing certain jobs. Company after company measures its people by these artificial standards. Eligibility for promotion reflects conformity, not results. And, more often than not, such company standards are implicit. A manager may be passed over for promotion not because of his or her results but because the way in which he or she operates diverges from certain unstated corporate expectations. I have worked with many corporate assessment centers and training programs. They are almost always based on an idealized view of job performance. Rarely do they acknowledge and build on the fact that individuals have unique ways of accomplishing outstanding performance.

Corporations base this common approach on a seemingly unassailable premise: that any job has very few peak performers and many mediocre ones. In an attempt to improve the caliber of the mediocre performers, companies study how the best performers function and then train everyone else to do the same job in the same way. This unassailable logic is in fact fallacious. When it is followed, it fills organizations with pale imitations of the few best. No one ever became an outstanding performer by imitating someone else. Imitation does have its place. It is an important foundation in the growth toward competency. Figure 4 illustrates the relationship between imitation and high performance.

Figure 4. Imitation and High Performance

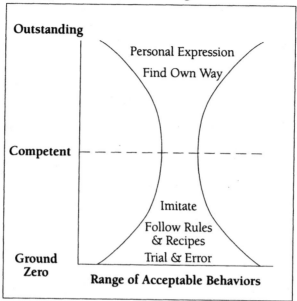

Getting Up to Competent

As Figure 4 shows, taking on any new job or activity necessarily involves a learning curve. You must progress from ground zero to competence. The standard techniques facilitate this learning process: Imitate someone more experienced and successful, follow simple rules and recipes, and use trial and error. These techniques are good, even essential. No one can achieve high performance without first mastering the basics and becoming competent.

Corporate training programs emphasize these basic techniques. The beginning courses in selling, for instance, give novices simple models to follow. Training in equipment diagnostics and repair starts with step-by-step lists. Introductory management courses teach delegating and performance review as a sequence of simple steps. Trainees who persevere with the learning process eventually become competent. The time between ground zero and competence varies with the job being learned. Sometimes it takes a month or two; sometimes it takes years. As employees move from trainee to competent performer, they develop shortcuts. Whatever the job, it takes less time than it did at first. At this point, most improvement levels off.

Note, however, that if we track the range of acceptable behaviors, the process of reaching competence is a process of reducing the range. Whatever the variety of behaviors that an untutored group has when it enters the process of becoming competent, its members will be a lot alike at the end. Everyone will learn to deal with the situation similarly.

Going from Competent to Outstanding

Contrary to general belief, everyone can move beyond competence to outstanding performance—if he or she knows how. Few actually make this transition consistently because the method for getting there is not the one by which they learned to be competent. Nobody tells them that the rules have changed. But the change is crucial.

In order to make the leap from competent to outstanding performer in any undertaking, you must incorporate all your knowledge and experience into your own unique way of being successful at that task. You have to step beyond the basic rules and recipes without forgetting them. You must move beyond imitation without losing your grasp of the fundamentals. As you make this transition, you create your own workable expression of your unique knowledge and skill. And it is this expression that makes you a high performer.

Uniqueness and Differences Are What's Important

Virtually every field of endeavor recognizes this simple fact: Outstanding people in any field have their own individually unique ways of working. A writer must find his own voice, a musician her own style of expression, a photographer his eye, an artist her style and medium. A simple analogy renders this crystal clear: If you listen to Van Cliburn, Andre Watts, and Arthur Rubenstein each perform the same piece of music, you will have three different musical experiences. Each artist expresses the music like no other.

This principle also applies in business. Think of the five best managers you have ever known, or the five best CEOs, or the five best salespersons. Why are they successful? It is true that at an abstract level there are always similarities between highly successful people. But what sets these extraordinary performers apart is their effective use of their unique qualities. People don't ever become really successful by imitating others.

PART I

Discovering High Performance Patterns

Over the years, I have found that if I just talk about High Performance Patterns, people are still full of questions. It is when I use real-life examples and describe the rigorous way in which we derive a pattern that many of the questions disappear. The actual case studies presented in this Part clarify what High Performance Patterns are and how radically they differ from other people-classifying approaches. Chapters 2 and 3 use authentic case studies to illuminate our process for discovering or identifying High Performance Patterns. In Chapter 4, I will answer some typical questions about High Performance Patterns.

Each chapter exemplifies how to use a pattern for very practical achievements. Keep in mind that we derive High Performance Patterns empirically. We analyze an individual's detailed stories of many diverse personal experiences of success. There is no predetermined notion of how a pattern should look. We never judge a pattern as good or bad. We merely attempt to record in minute detail what an individual actually did when he or she was the most successful. The resulting pattern shows the consistent, step-by-step sequence of actions underlying all the person's anecdotes. It simply delineates what the individual did to create each successful outcome.

Start with Better than Expected Experiences

We begin the search for High Performance Patterns with a deceptively simple process. We ask people to comb their personal history for experiences when, in their own judgment, they performed extraordinarily well. We define these as times when a project, activity, or relationship took off and went much better than anyone, especially the person telling the story, expected. Events from every arena of life are valid for this exploration. They need not reflect only the highest points, nor must they be limited to job experience.

Objectively important achievements and those of only personal significance are equally useful. For instance, if you consider both the time when you doubled your sales within a few months and the discussion that convinced your stepchild to work on improving a family relationship as high-performance experiences, they both qualify. You may even cite an event in which you feel you did superbly but no one else at the time thought so. Reasons for classifying such an event as successful often reveal great insights into a person's core values that help to pinpoint where behaviors can go off track.

Categories to Aid Recall

Most people remember their problems and failures more readily than they do their successes. Our recall process counteracts this tendency by helping people to identify times of past high performance. First, we ask people to think of categories of activities, such as job assignments, relationships, volunteer activities, recreation, and family events.

Next, we invite them to note any example that pops into mind in which an activity took off and succeeded beyond expectations. We place no limit on the amount of time involved in an experience—brief events lasting only a few hours and accomplishments requiring years are equally eligible. Nor do we predetermine the event's importance— the controlling criteria are the person's own judgment and definition of success. We encourage people to identify situations that they consider to have been successful even if no one else appreciated them and even if they occurred years ago. We even ask them to describe crises that they faced and handled much better than they expected. Everyone who refrains from prejudging his or her own examples as not good enough can recall quite a list—usually ten to fifteen events. Many of these are small experiences, virtually insignificant to anyone except the person who remembers them.

Representative Examples

After people list their high-performance experiences, we ask them to choose the three that are most alive, most representative of their very best. The three selected must come from markedly different circumstances. At least one must be a personal, nonbusiness example. When the person tells these three success stories in detail, we analyze them closely, looking for what happens consistently every time that the person achieves truly outstanding results.

Employ the Phases of High-Performance Experiences

We have identified four basic phases in every high-performance experience. In the first phase, the person becomes involved in an activity that will prove to be a high-performance experience. In the second phase, the person works to get the activity under way. The function of the third phase is sustaining the activity's momentum, keeping it together yet allowing it to develop in better than expected and unexpected directions. In the fourth and last phase, the person brings the activity to a solid, striking conclusion.

To help a person identify the common action steps in the three chosen stories, we suggest thinking of each story in terms of these four phases. We call them Getting Drawn In, Getting It Rolling, Keeping It Rolling, and Ending It Well.

Range of Individual Differences

Every person handles each phase in a unique way. We see enormous variations in approach and behavior among individuals. We have no preconceived notion of how any phase should look. Our goal is to identify the individual's own consistencies at each phase.

In the Getting Drawn In phase, some people always initiate. Others always have to be dragged in kicking and screaming. Some people plunge in with enthusiasm, not worrying about possible negative consequences. Others take their time, testing the waters carefully, and are ready to drop everything at the first sign of failure.

Some people handle the Getting It Rolling phase by careful and extensive advance planning. Others quickly sketch out how they'll do it and then act. Some don't plan at all. They try a number of things, building on whatever begins to work the soonest. Some scrupulously obtain permission from all the requisite authorities and line up all the needed resources in advance. Others make sure the activity is going strong before even informing the people who might say no.

Although the variations in the first two phases are extensive, we see an even wider range of successful approaches in the Keeping It Rolling phase. By this point, some people have delegated the activity, simply providing any residual needed guidance. Others stay in charge and relentlessly exhort everyone involved to greater and greater success. Some recruit new blood and new energy to keep the activity on a roll. Others consistently redouble their personal efforts to make sure that every detail is covered.

People also handle the Ending It Well phase in a variety of ways. Some remain involved to the bitter end, overseeing the project down to the last finishing touch. Others feel content and ready to move on as soon as a prototype proves to be viable. Some require solid evidence that their project has actually served its intended purpose and are not satisfied until they have hard evaluative data in their hands. For them the project is not complete until it has been analyzed in retrospect. Others relinquish a project without a backward glance.

Within this huge range of individual differences, each person follows a consistent pattern when he or she is being most successful. These are not better or worse ways of getting something done. They are unique ways of being successful. Each pattern works exceptionally well for the individual involved. Each person needs to find and understand what works for him or her.

Guiding Questions

To help this analytic process, we use a series of guiding questions for each phase. These questions focus the individual's attention on the relevant details in each story and stimulate exploration of the actions that are common to all the stories.

To give a sense of the direction that our guiding questions provide, in the Getting Drawn In phase, we ask how the person became aware of the activity, what risk-reward trade-offs attracted the person, and how he or she came to commit to doing it. We probe and push until ultimately we understand the steps of the process by which the person gets involved in an activity that ultimately becomes high performing.

For the Getting It Rolling phase, we ask how the person gathered information and generally decided what needed to be done, how he or she developed support from authorities and peers if not subordinates, and how he or she handled other aspects of the process of getting things organized for the main thrust of action. We probe and synthesize until we understand the steps of the process by which the person gets the activity under way.

For the Keeping It Rolling phase, we ask how the person reacted to initial successes or failures, his or her feelings at different points, whether he or she used outside experts, how he or she coped with pressure and problems, and whether mid-course corrections had to be made. We probe and cross-check to understand how the person keeps an activity rolling after it has gotten under way.

For the Ending It Well phase, we ask how the person ended his or her own involvement responsibly, how he or she was rewarded, and how he or she used the learning subsequently. After a great deal of mutual exploration, we end up with a good description of the steps that the person follows when he or she brings something to effective closure.

Probe for Deeper Insights and Connections

In every case, our guiding questions are just the beginning. Finding a High Performance Pattern is not a mechanical process. Merely answering a series of questions will not make your pattern emerge. It requires a mutual probing for increasingly deep insights into how a person works best and then a concerted effort to capture that process in a set of written steps. We never consider a pattern complete until the person really understands why the common elements in each high performance story work as well as they do. What does each step accomplish that moves the activity to the next stage until it ultimately concludes well?

I once worked with a vice president of a major computer company whose pattern illustrates the crucial importance of each action step and how each step sets the stage for the next one. Early in each of her high performance stories, this client got really angry with her boss. She virtually provoked him (she tended to have male bosses) into denouncing what she wanted to do. This action step in every high-performance activity was very upsetting. But she always returned to her boss afterward with an answer to every one of his objections. And those answers won his approval for her projects .

Eventually, she and I realized that this "provoking" step guaranteed that she would get honest feedback that she could use. Many women at her level find that colleagues are nice to them on the surface but vote against or undermine their proposed initiatives. Provoking her boss to anger was her effective way of finding out what she needed to know—what the authority figures actually thought about her work. Initially our client wanted to eliminate this painful and difficult step. But once she understood its purpose, she would not consider avoiding it.

Write the Pattern

In the final stage, we write out the step-by-step process in detail. Each individual then has a unique, personal guide to the way in which he or she achieves success. Each step in the completed pattern holds an insight about the person. Each step accomplishes something in an activity and sets the stage for the next step.

The detailed case studies in the next two chapters illustrate how we derive a pattern. In each chapter, you will meet an ordinary person who has had extraordinary success. You will hear the high-performance stories that revealed their High Performance Patterns. You will see what a completed High Performance Pattern looks like in written form. As you read, you will begin to understand how we discover High Performance Patterns, how we test them rigorously against the stories, and how perfectly the completed pattern fits the individual. You will hear in the person's own words how he or she made use of the pattern's insights to function more successfully.

The next two chapters present very detailed examples of the rigorous method by which High Performance Patterns are discovered. These are for those of you who like nitty-gritty detail. In spite of the somewhat pedantic presentation, such detail is useful to demonstrate how systematic and careful we are. For more readable examples, skip to Chapter 5.

2

Rebecca Allen's
High Performance Pattern

As prinicpal management analyst in the chief engineer's office of Rocky Mountain Water Company, Rebecca Allen has been the generalist on a management team of engineers for ten years. She is part of the management group that oversees a department of 300 employees in a division of 1,400. Rebecca's was a new staff position, which was defined when she was first hired. She coordinates engineering's annual operating and capital budget of $100 million for thirty-six units. This responsibility includes a six-month process of analysis and technical assistance with unit managers. Rebecca also works to improve management procedures, coordinates the annual management planning retreat, and, on the people side, looks for problems within the department and "things that can be made better."

Rebecca's Three High-Performance Stories

To start the discovery of her High Performance Pattern, Rebecca first recounted three stories of times when she had achieved results far better than she had originally anticipated.

The Capital Project Management System

Soon after I took the job, company management identified the need to design and implement a computerized capital project manage-

ment system, but the project was bogged down. I had minimal experience with such a massive project, but I knew all the key aspects of project development. I had worked with some of the key players on other assignments, and I saw this as a chance to work with a much wider management group. So I asked if others agreed with the need for the system, and then I asked to direct the project.

To develop the proposal, I set up a working task force representing each unit, and I hired a staff assistant. We took the conceptual plan that had been developed and dug into the tough analytic task of defining user requirements and thus the system design. Because users' requirements kept changing, I frequently touched base to monitor work tasks and keep the project team on track. I did some of the analytical work myself to be sure I had enough familiarity with the material and to ensure that we would use a common language. My staff assistant became the sounding board for reviewing any issues that arose, which we then resolved at our regular meetings.

We pulled out costs and benefits, looked at conflicting priorities, and discovered the limits of what a capital project management system could do for the company. At first, I accommodated too much, constantly accepting changing users' requirements, but I reassessed the situation after we had to redo a lot of detail work. Then I got all decisions grouped, reviewed by managers, and approved so that we could proceed with designing the system without worrying about redoing it. We discovered problems in every one of the available software packages, but we finally chose software and hardware that we believed could deal with the priorities that had emerged.

I presented the final proposal to the chief engineer with a recommendation that we retrench and proceed with the project on a much smaller scale. I concluded that it was far too massive an undertaking, with far too many unknowns, to go into full-bore. The chief engineer consulted with other managers in the department and decided to drop the project altogether, due to costs.

Management acknowledged the effort we had made and the importance of the data that I had gathered, particularly a critical-path analysis for major capital projects. I worked to get those data to people who could use them. I had my staff assistant document how far we had gone on the project before we separated on positive terms.

From a task perspective, the project might be considered a failure. But I have seen the data used frequently and recognized as a valuable contribution. Indeed, my analysis showed why the capital project management system project was ahead of its time, both in terms of what the division needed and in relation to costs. I have also applied what I learned to be sure that the scale and scope of other projects stay manageable from the start. I also know that the work laid a valuable foundation for developing a capital project management system in the future. Most important, I proved to myself and to others that I could play an invaluable leadership role on a complex project staffed by engineers and earn their respect. I was able to work effectively with many of them after that.

Making the Round Hill School Board Functional

My daughter had been a student at Round Hill, a private cooperative school, for three years. For the first couple of years, although I raised issues at co-op meetings and volunteered because I saw problems, nothing came of my efforts. The Round Hill School Board was made up of good people, but I felt they were allowing the school to deteriorate through inaction.

I tried to get elected to the board three times and finally won a seat the fourth time. My second year on the board, nobody wanted to be president—a symptom of the board's long-time problems—so I volunteered. Finally I had the authority to improve things. I announced my goals—for example, meetings no longer than two hours—and asked for others' goals. I did some very basic planning on issues—for example, what key issues needed discussion this meeting? which issues must be considered this year?—and led a discussion of the meeting format. I got folks to accept responsibility for what they were prepared to do or change, and we discussed the extent of our resources in terms of money and people.

Once the school year started, I found I had too much to do. We had money problems and limited numbers of people. I called on my past experience and visualized how meetings ought to go and how we could focus our efforts. I had regular conversations with the director and got her "permission" to moderate board meetings. I allowed people time to speak but sometimes cut people off to allow others to talk, and that garnered me support immediately. I got feedback from the board and staff, and both indicated success, with shorter meetings, more work produced, and more dollars invested, since the director now had time to do fund-raising.

In my daughter's last year of school, after six years on the board, I refused to be president again and refused to take a leadership role. Instead, I talked to people behind the scenes to influence issues and wrote a set of criteria for board decision making. It was difficult to leave because I had become so heavily invested in the board's success and the improvements at the school. Yet I knew that, because people need ownership to make a continuing program work, I had to break off from playing such a key role or none of it would last. Years later, I can see that I affected the board's decision-making process, although much of the substance of my work is no longer visible.

Flowers for the Acting Troupe

My seventeen-year-old daughter Tina called me at work one afternoon to say that she needed flowers for the teenage boys in her acting troupe for their performance that night. She had volunteered to get the flowers but hadn't done it, and now she had no time because she had to get to the theater. She added that she would prefer one rose for each boy. It was a typical last-minute, no-planning, teenage bailout request from Tina.

I realized that I was mad, that there was no time, and that I had no choice. I had to leave work at 4:30, commute home, get the flowers, and still have everything ready for Tina's troupe by 7:30 before the show started. I insisted on her okay to use my own judgment about what kind of flowers to buy.

I visualized small bouquets and tried to remember if I had tissue and ribbon at home. I called a couple of shops near my home for price estimates and decided to go to the grocery store for flowers because it was cheaper and closer. I called Tina back and told her that if she wanted my help, she could have no complaints. I asked *her for ideas and offered alternatives to roses. No problem. We agreed on blue irises.*

I got the flowers and worked furiously at home to get the bouquets together. When I brought them to the theater, Tina smiled and really thanked me. Most important, she didn't complain, and she actually seemed to understand that because of her irresponsibility she had caused me to do a lot of extra work and that she owed me some thanks for bailing her out. She even wrote me a brief thank-you note about it the next day. The troupe was all boys, and they were pleasantly surprised at both of us for giving them the flowers. The positive feelings lingered afterward. I thought, so that's the way to deal with Tina, by making an up-front agreement that she can't complain about what I do if she wants my help! Tina may not be responsible yet, but at least she won't take me for granted when I agree to help.

Developing Rebecca's High Performance Pattern

As outlined in the opening of Part I, to establish the specific steps of Rebecca Allen's High Performance Pattern, we examined her three stories in detail to determine the elements that they had in common. We used the four phases to look for the common sequence of events that occurs in all three stories: How did the stories start? That is, how did she get drawn in? How did she get things rolling? What did she do to keep things rolling? And, how did she end them well?

I asked Rebecca the series of guiding questions described earlier and probed her answers to isolate the common actions and conditions present in all her high-performance stories, cross-checking between stories until the pattern was clear. What emerged was a series of statements about how she works best—Rebecca's High Performance Pattern—that reflect and describe what she did every time she was highly successful.

Here is Rebecca's entire pattern. While you read it, get a sense of its sequence and flow. Notice how each single step leads into the next. This is what an action pattern should feel like. Individual steps in the pattern are numbered. It is followed by evidence from Rebecca's three success stories.

High Performance Pattern for Rebecca Allen

1. I perceive an opportunity to improve or upgrade a complex process involving overlapping issues and multiple people that is creeping along, causing a lot of gridlock.
2. I see a way to improve the relationships among the people involved (including myself) by doing it.
3. I get myself into a position to improve something by being asked to do it or by getting it assigned to me and agreeing to take it on.
4. I interview all the others involved to describe what I have in mind and to determine their ideas, agendas, and objectives, using my interpersonal skills to gain their trust and cooperation.
5. I pull my thoughts together into a draft plan and reach agreement with the others on the objective, the plan, and what the results will look like.
6. I lay out my conditions to do the task and get agreement from the powers-that-be for the independent authority and resources that I need. I offer in return to get it done and to have regular, straight communication.
7. I take on some of the actual work myself and ensure that others understand their tasks and roles by checking in with key people (individually and collectively) to keep information flowing.
8. I establish one other key person as a sounding board with whom I can review and brainstorm any issue and overall progress.
9. I go with my gut feelings whenever I have to assess priorities, plans, or work with others to make mid-course changes or other major decisions.
10. I keep balance in my life by maintaining several simultaneous activities and shift from one to another for renewal and perspective.
11. I stay with the project until the identified end objective is evident or the phase has run its course.
12. I take time to provide a transition for those who will maintain the process and implement the outcome.
13. I find I've been incorporated into and become an acknowledged part of the success of someone else, receiving thanks and recognition for my good work.
14. I assess, over time, the actual value of what I did, observe the applications, and consider how to do better the next time.

1. I perceive an opportunity to improve or upgrade a complex process involving overlapping issues and multiple people that is creeping along, causing a lot of gridlock.

Capital Management: Rebecca noted that the need for a computerized system was acknowledged, but the project had bogged down. The company required a very complex system for tracking its $100 million in projects. All segments of the division were concerned.

Round Hill: She saw problems at her daughter's school and raised them at board meetings for several years. She felt that the board was ineffective, and she had seen no satisfactory improvement.

Flowers for Teens: Rebecca had a long history of last-minute requests from her daughter to cover for the girl's irresponsibility, followed by complaints about the results. In the difficulty of rescuing her daughter at such short notice, Rebecca saw an opportunity to deal with their complex personal relationship.

2. I see a way to improve the relationships among the people involved (including myself) by doing it.

Capital Management: As a new staffer, Rebecca felt that pursuing the project would not only improve company operations but also increase her knowledge of Rocky Mountain systems and her credibility among the managers.

Round Hill: Rebecca felt that her organizational skills could be valuable to the school board, improving both board and school operations. Rather than be seen as a constant complainer, she could become a valuable resource for the school and get board members to work more effectively together.

Flowers for Teens: Rebecca saw an opportunity to change her relationship with her daughter while doing something for the teen actors.

3. I get myself into a position to improve something by being asked to do it or by getting it assigned to me and agreeing to take it on.

Capital Management: Rebecca asked for the project and got it assigned to her, although she had minimal experience with such massive endeavors.

Round Hill: She tried persistently to get elected to the board, failing three times before she won a seat. Then she was offered the president's role and accepted it.

Flowers for Teens: Rebecca agreed to meet her daughter's request.

4. I interview all the others involved to describe what I have in mind and to determine their ideas, agendas, and objectives, using my interpersonal skills to gain their trust and cooperation.

Capital Management: She interviewed managers to see whether they agreed that the computerized system was needed, and she interviewed task force representatives on users' needs. She clearly established herself as leader in the process and enlisted others as willing participants.

Round Hill: Rebecca asked for board members' goals and had regular conversations with the director, again establishing her role and getting others to welcome her in it.

Flowers for Teens: Rebecca "interviewed" her daughter, Tina, who preferred one rose for each player. After calling florists to see what was available at what cost, she used her interpersonal skills to discuss other options with Tina, and she gained Tina's agreement to trust her judgment and not to complain about the results.

5. I pull my thoughts together into a draft plan and reach agreement with the others on the objective, the plan, and what the results will look like.

Capital Management: She sorted out helpful input and got all decisions grouped for review by managers.

Round Hill: Calling on her past experience, Rebecca visualized how meetings would go and how the board could focus its efforts. She then led board members in a discussion of the limits on their resources in terms of money and people, until they adopted her action plan.

Flowers for Teens: Rebecca visualized small bouquets, then called her daughter to get an agreement on alternatives to roses. They agreed on irises.

> 6. I lay out my conditions to do the task and get agreement from the powers-that-be for the independent authority and resources that I need. I offer in return to get it done and to have regular, straight communication.

Capital Management: Rebecca got the authority to put together the task force and the resources needed to complete the planning phase. After we identified this step of her pattern, she realized that she could have obtained more explicit agreement for resources to develop the computerized system before she began work on the proposal.

Round Hill: She got the director's "permission" to moderate meetings, outlined her own goals, and got board members to accept responsibility for what they were prepared to do or to change.

Flowers for Teens: Rebecca got her daughter to agree that she could use her own judgment and that irises were an acceptable alternative to roses, and then established an understanding that there would be no complaints afterwards.

> 7. I take on some of the actual work myself and ensure that others understand their tasks and roles by checking in with key people (individually and collectively) to keep information flowing.

Capital Management: Rebecca did some of the analytical work herself and frequently touched base with the task force to keep them on track.

Round Hill: Rebecca moderated board meetings, took on responsibility for some activities, and monitored others at the meetings.

Flowers for Teens: She bought flowers at the grocery store, assembled the bouquets, and brought them to her daughter for distribution to the teenagers in the troupe.

> 8. I establish one other key person as a sounding board with whom I can review and brainstorm any issue and overall progress.

Capital Management: Rebecca's staff assistant became her sounding board.

Round Hill: The director became Rebecca's key person for review of issues.

Flowers for Teens: Rebecca's daughter was the key person.

9. I go with my gut feelings whenever I have to reassess priorities, plans, or work with others to make mid-course changes or
   other major decisions.

Capital Management: Rebecca accommodated too much at first. Then she reassessed the situation, sorted out helpful information, and took more control.

Round Hill: After realizing that she had too much to do and acknowledging that money and people were limited, Rebecca called on her past experience and visualized an alternative way to work.

Flowers for Teens: After pricing flowers, Rebecca judged that grocery store flowers would work and found alternatives to roses.

10. I keep balance in my life by maintaining several simultaneous
    activities and shift from one to another for renewal and per-
    spective.

Capital Management: Rebecca undertook this project in addition to her regular job responsibilities and continued to balance it with her regular work load.

Round Hill: This assignment was clearly an adjunct to regular work and home obligations.

Flowers for Teens: Rebecca made the initial calls from work and completed the project after she ended her regular workday.

11. I stay with the project until the identified end objective is evi-
    dent or the phase has run its course.

Capital Management: The chief engineer agreed with her recommendation to retrench but did not agree to pursue the project. Therefore, Rebecca disbanded her project team and terminated her staff assistant.

Round Hill: In the last year of her daughter's attendance at Round Hill, Rebecca began to back off. When Tina graduated, Rebecca ended her commitment to the board and the school.

Flowers for Teens: Once the flowers were delivered, the project was done.

12. I take time to provide a transition for those who will maintain the process and implement the outcome.

Capital Management: She worked to get the most useful data that emerged from the project to the people who could use them, and insisted that her staff assistant document the project.

Round Hill: Although she refused to be board president the last year, Rebecca talked to people behind the scenes and wrote the board to suggest decision-making criteria.

Flowers for Teens: Rebecca was able to help her daughter understand what had been involved in putting the bouquets together.

13. I find I've been incorporated into and become an acknowledged part of the success of someone else, receiving thanks and recognition for my good work.

Capital Management: Everyone, from task force members and managers to the chief engineer, acknowledged the value of Rebecca's project and recognized the validity of the data that she had developed.

Round Hill: Rebecca had become so heavily invested in the successes of the board at the school that it was difficult for her to transition out of her board work.

Flowers for Teens: Rebecca's daughter Tina smiled and thanked her when she saw the bouquets and later wrote a thank-you note. The teenage actors were pleasantly surprised by the flowers received from mother and daughter.

14. I assess, over time, the actual value of what I did, observe the applications, and consider how to do better the next time.

Capital Management: Over time, Rebecca continued to see that her work had laid a valuable foundation for developing a future capital management system. She also recognized that the data continue to be used.

Round Hill: Years later, Rebecca could see how she had affected the board's processes.

Flowers for Teens: Afterwards, Rebecca realized she had discovered a good way to deal with her teenage daughter by having Tina agree up front that she could not complain about what had been done if she wanted Mom's help.

Sequence and Linking of Steps

It is particularly important to note the sequence and linking among the steps in Rebecca's High Performance Pattern. Because the steps have been derived from the events in Rebecca's three success stories, events that take place in chronological order, the stories tell us which steps must precede the others. But if we want to use the pattern, we have to understand how the steps are linked—how completion of one step sets the stage for successful completion of a later step. For example, if Rebecca doesn't win people over with her skillful incorporation of their objectives (step 4), she will not be able to get their vital cooperation later. Similarly, if Rebecca does not get the up-front authority to act (step 6), her ability to take charge and drive the process will be much weaker later on. If she doesn't provide for a transition to others who will maintain the process that she has developed (step 12), the project will not end well. Each step in the process is essential. Rebecca will not be able to achieve success if any one step is omitted or performed badly. The early steps are particularly important, because they set the stage for the success of later steps.

Leverage Points and Activation Steps

As you can see, this pattern could not describe anyone other than Rebecca. The nuances are specific to her. Nobody is going to be successful in exactly the same way that Rebecca succeeds. And it is precisely the nuances that are important. If Rebecca is having trouble with something, it will be because she is off pattern somewhere in the sequence. In general, some early step will have been skipped or performed superficially.

Each statement in the pattern is written as a simple, factual description of an action step. To capture the nuances, we always attempt to include the individual's distinctive descriptive phrases. For example, the first step in Rebecca's pattern—perceive an opportunity to improve a complex process involving overlapping issues that is causing a lot of gridlock—catches how Rebecca described the common opening of her stories.

Rebecca's Pattern Characterized

Finally, we helped Rebecca to develop a short essence statement of her High Performance Pattern that briefly explained the way she did her best work in a way that was easy for her to remember. As Rebecca put it, "My High Performance Pattern is about unblocking complex processes that are creeping along and causing gridlock, by obtaining up-front authority, gaining the trust and cooperation of those involved, and putting in place a new process that is much better."

Rebecca's Reflections

"Two or three elements of my High Performance Pattern were revelations to me," Rebecca explained afterwards. "They were things that I had vaguely known about myself, but I had never put them into words, and I had not been aware of how critical they are to my performing at my best. For example, although I'm on the management team, I'm in a staff position, and I often need to get peers or superiors to agree explicitly that I have the authority and resources to complete a given project; that's the basis of a critical step (step 6) in my High Performance Pattern. Now I see the elements of my High Performance Pattern in many of the projects I work on, and I frequently remind myself of their importance so that I can do a better job!"

Rebecca chose to identify her own High Performance Pattern as part of a management development initiative. Over time, she determined that her pattern worked for her in a very practical way, and she suggested that having other department managers and staff work with their High Performance Patterns could be a catalyst for the group that would significantly enhance relations within work units.

Rebecca concluded that the process for defining High Performance Patterns would be particularly appealing to engineers, who are accustomed to following procedures carefully. As she put it, "The process is a natural for engineers, since it's derived from straightforward analysis." She also felt that, because the process doesn't delve into problems or deep psychological issues, it would be comfortable for relatively nonintrospective people.

"Working with my High Performance Pattern has increased my credibility and stature with management," Rebecca added, "and it has reinforced my confidence in myself. I find that my pattern provides an excellent tangible checklist that I can refer to. It helps me plan what I am going to do and check my progress."

3

Nick Rostov's
High Performance Pattern

Nick Rostov was human resources director at a large electronics company when I first identified and helped him apply his High Performance Pattern. Knowing his pattern helped Nick to reorganize personnel successfully so that human resources staff could become consultants to the company's operating divisions. Six years ago, in order to pursue his interest in linking human resources functions more tightly to the improvement of company operations, Nick used his pattern to cofound his present firm. Today, Nick Rostov is CEO of a thriving software company in the Atlanta area with thirty employees and $2 million in annual revenues that dominates the national market in a specialized software niche.

Nick Recalls Three High-Performance Stories

Nick began to identify his High Performance Pattern by recalling three times when he had achieved results far better than he had originally anticipated.

My Fantastic Racquetball Game After a Back Injury

All my life, I've wanted to be a good athlete, but I have never been naturally good. Because I needed some form of exercise, I took up racquetball, a sport that seemed something I could at least have a shot at doing well. I became very interested in it as a game, worked hard at it, read a lot about strategy, practiced all the different shots, and developed a complete game. After a while, through all my diligent and patient mastery of every aspect of the game, I became at least a competent player. I am very competitive and found I was only really excited when I was playing in a tournament or playing against someone who was better than me.

Then I had a back injury that set me back a lot. About six months after the injury, I was following my doctor's instructions and doing regular exercises, but there was constant low-level pain. I played racquetball irregularly, and my game deteriorated badly.

Then I played against a friend whom I used to be able to beat. I lost the first game but suddenly noticed that my back didn't hurt. I started playing much harder and much better, with the kind of concentration that I used to have. I focused on playing every point hard, concentrated on strategy, and tried to wear him down. I had a fantastic series of games. Everything worked, my back felt good, I won the second game and absolutely blew my friend away in the third. It was a real benchmark game.

Management Training Success with an Unfamiliar Audience in Belgium

I was twenty-nine. I had only recently come to work for the electronics company, and one of my first big responsibilities was designing and running a management training program in Europe. I badly wanted to do a good job, as it was my first opportunity to show what I could do, although it seemed way beyond my experience. I identified the topics to be covered, and I developed and made sure that each piece of the program was good. Then I put the pieces all together, and pilot tested the whole program twice in the United States. From that, I gained some confidence that it was a good program.

But I was still terrified. They were flying me to Belgium and bringing in managers from all over the continent. I was intrigued by how European management worked, but I had not spent enough time in Europe to understand how management worked there. I wasn't at all certain that ideas that worked in the United States would be effective overseas.

I remember spending the day before the training asking questions of everyone, hoping to get a handle on the nature of management in Europe and how it differed from ours in the United States. I fell asleep playing the seminar over and over in my mind, and I got up during the night to check and recheck everything in the training room.

The next day, the seminar went beautifully. It was like a dance for three days. I was able to accomplish much more than I ever thought. The managers responded well, I was asked to come back, and afterwards I was on an incredible high.

In the years since, I have taken every chance to talk to people from the seminar, just to see whether the concepts were really helpful. At one point, I almost went to Europe to work for six months, so I could understand how business there works.

Successful Speech for Admission into the High School Senate Club

In the 1963–64 school year, before Martin Luther King led the march on Washington and before the civil rights legislation of the Lyndon Johnson years, I had to give a prepared speech as a final test for admission into my high school's Senate Club. The club was run like the United States Senate, and members debated various bills. I was very nervous, as I had never given a speech before and certainly not one that was to be judged. I very much wanted to get into the club.

My topic was integration and affirmative action. I got intrigued by the topic. I researched it thoroughly, identified all the different threads of the topic, and became fascinated by putting them all together into an argument. I planned the speech carefully, wrote it and rewrote it until it was a very tight, elegant package. For example, the speech opened and ended with the same line, and ended with an emotional crescendo. I practiced it in front of my mother several times. When I finally started the speech at the Senate Club,

I began to get the response I wanted early on, and I just kept build-ing on it. My speech was a smashing success, and I got into the Senate Club.

Identifying Nick's High Performance Pattern

To identify Nick's High Performance Pattern, we followed the proce-dure that I outlined in the beginning of Part I. We examined his stories in detail. We looked for the sequence of actions and events common to all three stories. I asked Nick our guiding questions about many dimensions of each experience, using the four phases: How did he get drawn in? How did he get things rolling? What did he do to keep things rolling? And how did he end them well?

I probed Nick's answers to isolate the common actions and condi-tions present in all his success stories, cross-checking between stories until his pattern emerged clearly. As with Rebecca, what surfaced was a series of statements about how he worked best—Nick's High Perfor-mance Pattern—that described the precise sequence of steps Nick always follows when something he does works extraordinarily well.

Nick's complete written High Performance Pattern appears on the opposite page. Following is each step of the pattern along with evi-dence from Nick's three high-performance stories.

> 1. I get engaged with an activity I have not done before that gives me a chance to show how well I can do, and I want to do it well.

Racquetball: Nick wanted to become a good athlete but lacked natural talent. He chose racquetball, feeling that he had a chance to become pretty good at it.

Management Training: Nick was new to management training but badly wanted to demonstrate what he could do. Designing and delivering a European training program gave him an opportunity to prove his abilities.

Senate Club Speech: Nick had never given a speech before. Ap-plying for the Senate Club would give him a chance to show how well he could do. A good speech would get him into the Senate Club.

High Performance Pattern
for Nick Rostov

1. I get engaged with an activity I have not done before that gives me a chance to show how well I can do, and I want to do it well.

2. I recognize that "tests" are an inherent part of the activity and that ultimately what I do will be put to a significant test that I'm not sure I can pull off.

3. I start it, find that getting good at it intrigues me, and get completely drawn into it.

4. I identify every aspect of the activity and work on mastering them one at a time until I understand how to exploit their possibilities fully.

5. I weave all the strands together into the best model I can create for the requirements of the situation.

6. I recognize there is an unknown or uncontrollable element that adds uncertainty to the outcome and heightens my concentration.

7. I pilot test and refine the model until it is elegant and polished.

8. I give the model the ultimate test, running it just as planned, and it works fabulously, building to an incredible crescendo.

9. I receive clear, positive test results that show how well I've done.

10. I feel satisfied that I have proved my ability and deserve to play at the new level of accomplishment.

2. I recognize that "tests" are an inherent part of the activity and that ultimately what I do will be put to a significant test that I'm not sure I can pull off.

Racquetball: Nick was not sure he could be a good athlete. Racquetball involves built-in interim tests to measure his progress—winning or losing games against increasingly tough opponents. Eventually Nick would know whether he could achieve his athletic goals.

Management Training: The written evaluations submitted after every presentation of his management training program would have to reflect positively on Nick. If not, his work would be judged a failure. Initially, he was not convinced he could pull it off.

Senate Club Speech: The club would base its vote to admit or refuse Nick on the quality of his speech. He was not positive when he started that he could meet its standards for admittance.

3. I start it, find that getting good at it intrigues me, and get completely drawn into it.

Racquetball: Nick soon found that racquetball was within his capabilities, and he became intrigued with mastering its intricacies.

Management Training: Adapting management training to European business intrigued Nick and soon captivated his attention.

Senate Club Speech: Nick was intrigued by integration and affirmative action and researched his topic scrupulously.

4. I identify every aspect of the activity and work on mastering them one at a time until I understand how to exploit their possibilities fully.

Racquetball: Nick worked on each racquetball stroke until he developed a complete game. He studied strategy until he could plan how to beat an opponent.

Management Training: Nick identified all of the topics to be covered. He developed each in turn, making sure that the separate parts were good before combining them.

Senate Club Speech: Nick identified and understood each thread of the topic thoroughly before he developed his presentation.

5. I weave all the strands together into the best model I can create for the requirements of the situation.

Racquetball: Nick developed an overall model of strategy and individual game plans. He practiced particular strategies in preparation for particular opponents. When he found that his back didn't hurt, he executed the plan that he had used previously to beat this opponent and won.

Management Training: He combined all the topics into a coherent training program.

Senate Club Speech: Nick built a tightly woven argument from all his topic threads. His speech opened and ended with the same line and built to an emotional crescendo.

6. I recognize there is an unknown or uncontrollable element that adds uncertainty to the outcome and heightens my concentration.

Racquetball: He wasn't really sure that his back would hold up long enough to allow him to beat his opponent.

Management Training: He wasn't sure that the European managers would listen to him or that the training program, good as it might be for the United States, would be relevant to European management conditions.

Senate Club Speech: He was himself a member of an ethnic minority, and he wasn't sure how that would affect the vote on his speech.

7. I pilot test and refine the model until it is elegant and polished.

Racquetball: Before he hurt his back, Nick practiced his racquetball game against many opponents. Each opponent was a pilot test for the next. He knew the approach that would beat this particular opponent. He just wasn't sure he was physically able to carry it off.

Management Training: He pilot tested the management program twice in the United States before taking it to Europe.

Senate Club Speech: He practiced his speech several times in front of his mother before giving it at the Senate Club.

8. I give the model the ultimate test, running it just as planned,
   and it works fabulously, building to an incredible crescendo.

Racquetball: Nick had been able to beat this opponent regularly before his injury, so playing against him was an accurate gauge of Nick's recovery. During the match, Nick's game improved progressively, until he finally blew his opponent away.

Management Training: The European managers responded positively almost from the outset and accepted Nick's training program without reserve. By the time they completed final formal evaluations, Nick's success was a foregone conclusion.

Senate Club Speech: The Senate Club members responded positively to Nick's speech from the very beginning. He built on that response for a powerful ending.

9. I receive clear, positive test results that show how well I've
   done.

Racquetball: Nick beat his friend convincingly in the second racquetball game and blew him away in the third.

Management Training: The European managers praised Nick highly in the formal evaluations and invited him back.

Senate Club Speech: The Senate Club voted him in.

10. I feel satisfied that I have proved my ability and deserve to
    play at the new level of accomplishment.

Racquetball: Nick was satisfied that he was playing much harder and better. He used his victory to measure his recovery from the back injury. He never even mentioned beating his friend as part of the goal when he told the racquetball story.

Management Training: Nick never worried again about whether he deserved his job. He knew he had proved himself.

Senate Club Speech: When the members voted to admit him, Nick knew he really belonged. He had demonstrated his ability.

Sequence and Linking of Steps

As we saw in Rebecca's pattern, the sequential linking of steps is particularly important. The stories tell us which steps must precede others. Using a pattern requires understanding how completion of one step sets the stage for successful completion of a later step.

To achieve high performance, Nick must engage in an activity that lets him show how well he can do. If he can't ultimately demonstrate a high level of competence through both interim and final tests, he will not operate in High Performance Mode. Nick does not do his best work in fuzzy, unclear environments. Nick's high-performance activity must also be something he can master methodically, one piece at a time, at his own pace, before doing anything major with it. If he has to function quickly in an environment about which he knows little, he won't be in high-performance mode.

Nick's mastery sequence is crucial. In high-performance mode, he always constructs a model and then tests it. If he hasn't mastered all the individual segments, he can't construct his model. Without his model, he can't assess his mastery, and he won't feel that he deserves to operate at the new level. Isolated victories don't do it for Nick. Creating and testing an elegant model and proving that it works is how he demonstrates true mastery.

Leverage Points and Activation Steps

The pattern just outlined could not describe anyone other than Nick, any more than Rebecca's could describe someone other than Rebecca. The nuances are too specific to him. These nuances are key. If Nick has trouble succeeding at something, it will be because he is off pattern somewhere in the sequence. This usually means that some early step was skipped or performed superficially.

To capture these crucial nuances, we include people's distinctive descriptive phrases in their pattern statements. For example, Nick repeatedly used the expression *get intrigued* to describe the conditions that drew him into intense work to make something succeed. We used those words verbatim in his pattern. Without first getting intrigued, Nick does not produce his best work.

Nick's Pattern Characterized

Finally, we developed a short statement of Nick's High Performance Pattern that captured the essence of how he worked best, one that he could remember easily. As he put it, "My High Performance Pattern is about proving my ability to play at a new level of accomplishment by mastering each aspect of the activity, creating the best model I can, and receiving hard proof that my model works fabulously in the ultimate test situation."

Nick's Reflections

When Nick reflected on his pattern, he realized that he already knew most of it. But having it written down and validated gave him much more confidence to face new situations and make choices. Like Rebecca, some insights surprised him—that he liked entering new situations, that he mastered them in pieces, and that testing models was a way of demonstrating mastery. These insights also told Nick something deeper about himself—that after mastering all aspects of a project and creating and testing his model, he would need a new activity to grow into. Unless his environment included periodic new challenges, Nick would move on regularly.

4

Answers to Typical Questions About Discovering Patterns

As you can see from the chapters on Rebecca and Nick, we distill High Performance Patterns rigorously from the actual stories that our clients tell us. We have clients carefully identify and recount a large number of personal incidents in which some activity has taken off and gone better than expected. They select three incidents (either two business and one personal or one business and two personal) that they feel represent them at their best. With the client, we scrutinize each of these primary stories phase by phase, using our guiding questions to identify the common actions and conditions generating the person's successes.

Now that the examples of Nick and Rebecca have made you familiar with our process, I can address some questions that people often ask when we introduce the concept to them.

1. *Three stories don't seem like a very solid basis on which to develop a pattern. If three other stories were picked, wouldn't the pattern be quite different?*

As you saw with Nick and Rebecca, we always use three primary stories. But keep in mind that the client generates many more than three high performance stories during our consultations. As the pattern takes shape, we check it against the person's other anecdotes. Any time a secondary story suggests ways in which the draft pattern can be refined, we relentlessly cross-check it with the three primary stories. This process leads to a high degree of consistency and refinement. The pattern that eventually emerges is crystal clear. We always make sure that it is consistent with all the person's high-performance examples. Until a pattern is truly consistent, we do not consider it to be complete. A pattern consistent with many past high-performance examples is an eminently solid basis on which to plan future activities.

2. *Couldn't someone fake a High Performance Pattern or make it come out the way he or she wanted to by inventing stories?*

It's possible. But it would be extremely difficult—far more difficult than giving dishonest answers to the multiple-choice questions on the standardized, computer-scored tests that many other characterizing methods use. To fabricate a pattern, a person would have to invent multiple richly detailed stories in a variety of settings and make sure that all had the same underlying pattern of actions that the analysis was to uncover. Because no client knows how we analyze the stories until later in the process, this would be extremely difficult. And actual high-performance stories reflect real life in all its richness and unpredictable detail, a very hard thing to duplicate. Authors and actors know that writing or speaking convincing fiction is so hard precisely because truth is always stranger than fiction. Although I am a trained actor and writer, I find it extremely difficult to make up high-performance stories consistent with someone else's pattern. To be convincing, I always have to use their actual stories when talking about them.

Perhaps even more germane is the question, Why would someone even want to create a fake pattern? The High Performance Pattern is, after all, how someone works best. Your authentic pattern is one of the most useful things that you can know about yourself—not only for you but for those who work with you. Someone might want to create an inaccurate self-presentation. But if others base cooperative efforts and working relationships on that false pattern, it will soon become apparent that something isn't working. None of us can really run from who we are. And we don't need to run from who we are at our best!

Nonetheless, some people do find aspects of themselves in their High Performance Patterns that they don't like at first. They want to change those, just as Warren initially wanted to change his procrastination. However, by completing the process, they learn to see and to value why those aspects of their patterns work. Others start the process convinced that, if their organization understood their real pattern, they would be fired. These people try to appear as they think their organization requires them to be. But once the strengths embedded in their patterns are seen as the assets they really are, the organization almost always values them more highly and deploys them in ways more appropriate to their strengths.

> 3. *Why do you work only with what the person tells you? Aren't people going to give much more glowing accounts of their roles and contributions in their stories than any objective observer would agree is true? Aren't patterns going to be little more than idealized portraits?*

It is true that a person's High Performance Pattern has a certain mythic hero quality. Patterns are intended to be pictures of people at their very best. The reality that most of us operate less effectively than we can—at least before we know our pattern—does not change the fact that each of us is capable of much more. Comparing high performance with normal performance is like comparing a machine's best possible performance with its actual performance. Ideal pictures illuminate what needs to change to bring actual performance in line with potential. Thus, clear descriptions of the best possible outcome are extremely useful in many areas of human endeavor, even if the reality often falls short.

Granted that, there is a certain degree of exaggeration in high-performance stories. What happens if it is so out of proportion to reality that the resulting pattern is unreal and impossible to follow? Some other approaches to identifying personal characteristics address this problem: For example, people can give questionnaires to their colleagues, friends, and bosses. The responses underline the divergence between how others view them and how they view themselves. I don't want to downplay the value of this independent feedback. Evaluation and confirmation of your self-perception gives you a necessary and objective reality check.

We encourage people to show their patterns to those who know them, particularly those involved in their high-performance stories, and ask for feedback. Two very good things often result. First, the people to whom our clients show their patterns almost always confirm the overall pattern. These friends and colleagues tend to appreciate seeing the pattern—it helps things fall into place for them. The ensuing discussions are usually very positive and rewarding. Second, by discussing the stories' nuances, as clients often do when they show their patterns to others, they often remember them more accurately. Then they can fine-tune their patterns. We believe in a confirmation process involving others who participated in the events that the stories recount.

Although we encourage people to get feedback, we prefer that they ascertain their High Performance Patterns before they get reactions to them. Getting feedback in advance is impractical. High-performance stories are often of past events in widely divergent places involving people with whom the client is no longer associated. Since high-performance stories are as unique as the experiences that they recount and the people who tell them, there is no standard set of questions to ask. The client would have to write out the stories in great detail and then share them with others who were there.

The ultimate corrective to possible exaggeration is the actual use of the pattern. We do not regard a pattern as a definitive "being" statement about a person. A pattern is a living tool. It is meant to be used as an empowering personal guide to ways of being more effective in the world. If a pattern has serious flaws, it won't work as a guide. Lines of action based on it will run into trouble.

When a pattern has flaws, we always recommend going back and looking more closely at the stories on which the pattern was based. Usually an overlooked element of the stories suggests a refinement in the pattern that corrects the problem. The full truth always resides in the actual high-performance stories. The written pattern is only the set of steps derived from their content to account for past successes and thereby guide future action.

At the beginning, we prefer that people work only with their own memories and assessments of their worth and contributions. Most people have been so buffeted by problems, negative feedback, and other people's opinions about them that they have lost confidence in their own choices and judgments. To be truly empowered, they must correct this tremendously debilitating condition. To achieve high-performance results, someone carrying out complex activities must be confident in making personal judgments and taking action in the moment. Because we expect and encourage clients to assert their own value and to claim their own contributions from the start, people who begin by attempting to trick the process so it produces a pattern they think others want eventually realize that they have tricked themselves. Once they grasp the concept of personal empowerment, they search for real insights about themselves.

4.   *Is each pattern really unique?*

Yes. The detail in each pattern step and the reliance on the individual's actual language in telling and analyzing the stories guarantee that their two patterns will never be identical. Of course, there are significant similarities among patterns. You can group and classify patterns. For instance, you can identify a group of salespeople whose patterns show them to be great at getting things started. It would be reasonable to pool them as adept at opening new sales situations. You can isolate another group as adept at finishing things and pool them as the good closers. But what is gained and what is lost by this grouping and categorizing? In my view, categorizing undermines virtually everything of importance about patterns.

Grouping and categorizing is the major methodology on which academia relies. But in order to group things, you have to ignore many individual nuances. And it is precisely those individual nuances that empower particular individuals to do their best work. Sam may be an opener, but in order to help Sam lay out a plan for opening the Ajax account, you need detailed knowledge of Sam's best way of working and not anyone else's. Jane may be a closer, but to help her close a sale at Barney Products, you need detailed knowledge of Jane's best way of working, not anyone else's. Categories don't help.

The same is true if either Sam or Jane is involved in some activity that isn't working well. Knowing that Sam is a good opener doesn't help to identify what Sam is doing wrong—it's too general. But knowing in detail how Sam does things when he works best will help. Knowing Jane's type or style doesn't help. Individual details of how

Jane works best will. Patterns are unique. Moreover, it is precisely this uniqueness that helps people to consistently achieve high levels of performance.

5. *Isn't a significant portion of high performance just luck? Surely I can't just reproduce my best any time and every time I want.*

High performance is not and never will be mechanical. Producing outstanding results can involve a significant degree of luck or serendipity. And just as athletic teams can have off days, an activity may sometimes not jell, even with high-performance factors in place. But many people, out of ignorance, do not even try to create the conditions that they need in order to produce outstanding work. They continue to plug along, with significant frustration and lack of impact, using techniques and approaches that don't fit them.

Knowing what to change to get the right fit will produce an improvement over the results of working badly off pattern, even if the ultimate results are totally outstanding. The process itself will be far more energizing. And following your pattern maximizes the potential for things to go better than expected. Using your High Performance Pattern puts you in a state of readiness for outstanding achievement.

6. *Does your High Performance Pattern change?*

As far as we can tell, the principle features of a person's High Performance Pattern are remarkably stable, at least from age thirty on. In many cases, the major elements of an individual's pattern are evident at much younger ages. We know this because we encourage people to pick a few high performance stories from earlier periods in their lives. Many can identify one from teenage years. One client had a vivid memory of a high-performance experience from age six or seven. Examples from military service and college are commonplace. People in their forties and fifties who find their patterns and then test them against examples from their teens and early twenties are often amazed to see how consistent the pattern has been. It often matches their earlier experiences like a glove.

People have repeated our program after as many as seven years, finding their pattern the second time without reference to the first. The consistency between first and second patterns is remarkable.

Although the person's exact wording inevitably changes, the principal elements remain the same.

However, patterns are not static. They grow richer in detail and nuance as life experiences accumulate. Adults are the same people they were as children but physically, mentally, and emotionally matured. Patterns mature, too, but retain their essential elements. Your ability to succeed grows as you gain experience in a wider variety of situations. Your pattern grows with you. You still approach situations in the same way, but the way you execute individual steps reflects your level of maturity.

Let's imagine that one step in "Mike's" High Performance Pattern is to plan carefully how to proceed before he initiates action. As Mike gains experience, his planning skills improve. He develops his own ways of determining what an activity needs and of making better plans. He takes courses in planning and, by learning to use sophisticated state-of-the-art techniques, improves even more. Mike's planning competence grows and changes as he does. But he still plans. It is unlikely that he will produce outstanding work if he drops the step of planning carefully, no matter how skilled he becomes as he grows older.

7. *Is it possible to produce outstanding work and not follow your pattern?*

Yes. But you will do it in grind-it-out mode, which can be extremely costly in terms of burnout and exhaustion. Producing outstanding results when you are off pattern usually means that you have no excitement or upbeat energy. Your method cannot be sustained, because it doesn't really fit you. Some of our most poignant clients are people who have been paid very well for a long time to do something fundamentally off pattern for them. By the time they come to us, they are suffering profoundly—unhappy, stressed out, drinking too much, struggling with a troubled marriage, and so on. When you're on pattern, the rightness about the work and the way you go about it means that you handle any accompanying stress positively.

8. *Aren't some patterns better than others? Can't I change mine for a better one once I know it?*

No, some patterns are not inherently better than others. By definition, every High Performance Pattern works effectively for the individual whom it fits. Each individual's unique skills, abilities, training, and experience determine what challenges can handled successfully.

Some patterns are more naturally suited to certain activities than to others. Mike's pattern depends in part on careful planning. It is not naturally suited for situations that develop rapidly. For that reason, Mike's pattern would be of little use in fighting a forest fire on the front line or landing a crippled airplane. In contrast, "Marti" might have a crisis-handling pattern. She would be on pattern in such situations. Nevertheless, careful planning can be an advantage even in crisis situations—if it means getting advance training on how to handle all possible contingencies. With adequate preparation, Mike could be on pattern in such situations, and it seems likely that he would still be one of the most valuable participants precisely because his ability to plan is unusual in a crisis situation.

To change—or attempt to change—a pattern from what it is to something it isn't seems not to work. Remember how hard it was for Warren to stop procrastinating? When he wrote his speeches the "right" way, he was off pattern. The quality dropped significantly. It was only when Warren used what truly worked for him that he produced outstanding work. In the same way, it would be very difficult for our imaginary friend Mike to be outstandingly effective at winging it, particularly when competing with someone like Marti. And an outstanding improviser like Marti would have trouble getting really good at planning. Marti naturally produces outstanding work when she wings it. Extensive advance planning is not likely to improve her results.

So don't consider changing your pattern—improve it by getting better at each step. If you are a planner, train yourself in planning techniques. If you persuade others to do something as part of your pattern, study and become skilled at persuasion techniques.

9. *How much of my pattern do I already know?*

Quite a bit. Depending on your age, it's very unlikely that much of your pattern will come as a complete surprise. In order to be as successful as you have already been, you must already have some knowledge of what works for you.

Individual elements of a pattern rarely surprise our clients. What often surprises them is the fact that a pattern exists. Sometimes people know their pattern in general, but they are unaware of one or two items, or have them backwards. For example, someone thinks that she does her best work persuading people to follow her. In fact, she is so sure that she's right that she doesn't listen to anyone who needs persuasion. People follow her not because she persuades them to, but because they know she is likely to get where she says she's going. Understanding the real dynamic of your success gives you great confidence—you can avoid wasting time trying techniques that wouldn't work for you anyway.

Many people discover that certain steps in their pattern are the key ones. If they get those key elements in place, the rest tend to follow. Precisely because they are crucial, the key steps are the ones where the person is most likely to go off pattern. Even if you already know most of your pattern, identifying your key steps is extremely valuable.

10. When are patterns formed?

We don't know. Psychologists maintain that the major elements of a pattern take primitive shape very early—perhaps by the time of toilet training. Several members of the clergy who know of our work feel that each individual is probably born with a pattern. It represents God's plan for the person.

No matter how early a pattern forms, our methodology for determining it requires people to identify high-performance stories that capture them at their unique best. Therefore, we are reluctant to determine a High Performance Pattern for someone younger than his or her mid twenties. A client must have enough life experience and a sufficiently developed personality to distinguish stories and behavior that truly illustrate his or her unique characteristics from behavior born of peer group pressure or the influence of parents, teachers, or religious affiliation.

11. How are High Performance Patterns different from other ways of describing and classifying people?

There are many ways of describing and classifying people. Many start by asking people to recall times when they did something well. They then analyze those events to produce insights. Bernard Haldane (1974) perfected this approach to career counseling many years ago. Virtually all career counseling and outplacement methods have followed suit. The ever-popular *What Color Is Your Parachute?* (Bolles, 1990) is based on it.

The High Performance Pattern approach selects a far more refined set of examples. We don't ask just for times when someone did something well. We ask for times when something went better than expected. The distinction may seem minor. In fact, it is major. The distinction between *do exceptionally well* and *go better than expected* yields markedly different anecdotes from the same person.

The essence of high performance is this phenomenon of having the activities take off. It distinguishes outstanding results attained simply by working exceptionally hard (what we call *grinding it out*) from true high performance. True high performance almost always seems easy and effortless. And to understand high performance, the examples must be not simply of outstanding results but of results achieved through this essential phenomenon.

In contrast to other approaches, we work only with the experiences that our individual client deems to be high performance. This is why we get examples that the rest of the world would judge to be failures. Even these examples reveal what has meaning for the person. Requests to identify something that the person did well tend to produce examples based on the external world's assessment of the result. Many of these examples are actually destructive to the process. A lawyer with whom we worked could have listed many cases that he had won. The external world certainly judged them as things that he had done well. Yet the only high-performance examples that he produced from his work involved cases that he had lost. They revealed much more about what really provided meaning and motivation to him than any of the cases that he had won. Other approaches would rarely have uncovered such examples.

We describe a person's entire success process from beginning to end. Other approaches look for common themes, specific but isolated insights (for example, *you like working with people, not with things*) or lists of strengths and weaknesses (for example, *you are good at numbers; you like being a devil's advocate*). These insights are not bad or wrong—they are just incomplete. Seeing the whole success process within which these action are embedded makes it clear that these isolated insights are true only part of the time, during a certain phase of the entire process. For example, the executive of the high-tech firm whom I described in the beginning of Part I provoked her boss to anger, but she was not argumentative and provoking all the time. She used that skill only at one point in her pattern and for one purpose—to get honest feedback.

One of our clients, a middle-level manager, was so good at handling details that his company always assigned him very detailed work. He found this work unsatisfying. When we uncovered his full pattern, he found that he was good at handling details to get them out of the way so that he could concentrate on longer-term strategic thinking. His real strength was in building a program strategically over a number of years. Because his company had categorized and rewarded him only for one isolated strength without knowing the role that it played in his whole pattern, our client had been so overburdened with detailed work that he had no time to strategize, nor could he stay with a project for the long term. As you can see, understanding the whole process of succeeding is crucial.

Patterns describe a whole process over time. Most other systems simply group and classify people. Instead of making an individual point-by-point comparison of someone's actions with the steps in his or her unique High Performance Pattern, they relegate the person to a type of group and attempt to diagnose and prescribe corrective action based on the group's characteristics. Classification schemes are ubiquitous. I have seen a plethora of four-cell personality classification schemes (*supporter, promoter, analyst,* and *driver,* for example), numerous others schemes for management styles, seven categories of "problem" people, and so on.

The most widely used of these schemes and in many ways the most complex is the Myers-Briggs Type Indicator (MBTI) system. Based on the work of Carl Jung, it divides people into one of sixteen basic categories (four dimensions with two types per dimension). David Kiersey and Marilyn Bates wrote an entire book, *Please Understand Me* (1984), to explain the meaning and characteristics of each category. Interpretation of the MBTI requires considerable expertise.

Among its limitations, people are not distributed evenly among its various categories. Two types, INFP and INTP, apply to only 1 percent of the general population. Several others are seen only rarely in corporate settings. Consequently, the scheme has less power to differentiate among people in a given corporate situation than it seems to. And like other approaches, MBTI treats individuals as members of groups, which means that it necessarily discounts individual nuances among members of the same group. But individual nuances are the key to getting the very best work out of someone.

Since the MBTI is so widely used, we have done considerable work matching High Performance Patterns with MBTI categories. We used the patterns of individuals for whom we also had the Myers-Briggs type. We brought together a number of MBTI experts to rate and discuss patterns. When we tried rating and classifying the individual steps within a pattern, the person bounced all over the MBTI map. One step indicated one type, the next a different type, and so on. It just didn't work.

We asked the experts to classify entire patterns. They reached consensus on individual patterns, but each pattern had segments that didn't fit the Myers-Briggs classification of the whole. When we tried classifying each phase (Getting Drawn In, Getting It Rolling, Keeping It Rolling, and Ending It Well), the experts had much more success. Each phase in a person's pattern fits a Myers-Briggs type. But many people's Myers-Briggs types change from phase to phase. You can be one type when getting drawn in, another when you get something started, still another when you keep something going, and a fourth when bringing something to a close.

We concluded that High Performance Patterns go beyond even the most sophisticated classification scheme in significant ways. The most important of these is that patterns describe an entire process taking place over a period of time that results in a successful outcome. All classification schemes are necessarily static in time, and therefore they cannot hope to represent an entire success process accurately. They are more like a note or a chord, while patterns represent the tune or the entire musical score. Finally, patterns describe individual uniqueness. Sixteen cells are a crude measure when we compare them with thousands or even millions of people whose individual differences are what really account for their best performances.

12. Can I find my own High Performance Pattern?

We encourage anyone who wants to to try. Make a list of the times when you've had the experience of having something take off and go better than expected. Select three or more different stories, and write them out in detail. Spend some time analyzing them. Note the actions that were common to every story and see if you can put them into a sequence that feels right to you. Then show the resulting pattern to people who know you, preferably people who were part of the experiences that you have used as your examples. Ask them for feedback. Then try your pattern out and see if it works.

Although you can conceivably find your pattern on your own, I urge you to spend some time with someone has been trained in finding patterns and who has done hundreds of them. There are a number of reasons for this. First we all have certain blind spots. By definition, it takes someone else to identify them. A blind spot will show up in your self-developed pattern as a missing step. And a missing step means that you can't truly function on pattern.

In addition, unless you are a very secure and open person, your first reaction to any aspects of your pattern that reveal something you haven't wanted to admit about yourself are likely to be negative. A trained person can help you understand the positive virtue in something that you have assumed to be negative (for example, procrastination, provoking people to anger).

Finally, basing a course of action on your pattern involves a creative process—thinking through what activating your pattern in a specific situation means. It helps to brainstorm with another person, particularly if you are in a troubling situation. Neither Rebecca, nor Nick, nor many of the other people you will read about in this book could have come up with their creative breakthroughs without some discussion with someone else. Patterns enable someone else to help you think through your situation within your own frame of reference. For that alone, they are well worth the effort.

PART II

Applying High Performance Patterns

When a machine is not operating well, we turn to the manual that came with it for a description of its optimal performance. By comparing our data on the machine's actual performance with the specifications in the manual, we can diagnose what's wrong and determine what to do about it.

Even well-made machines are not identical. One machine may run best a few degrees hotter or a few degrees colder than the manual says. For best output, the pressure may need to be higher on one machine than on others. Good engineers add their own notes accounting for quirks and special characteristics to the manual for each piece of equipment that they use.

Patterns as the Standard of Comparison

Each individual's unique High Performance Pattern functions as that person's manual. People are far more complex than machines—one manual will not apply to everyone. Each of us needs his or her own. Although each of us has a different manual, we can use them in similar ways. Your own pattern of success is always the best standard with which to compare your current actions and find ways of improving results.

Principal Applications

Patterns have three broad uses: problem solving, planning, and choosing among alternatives. When a project in which you are involved is not going well, you can use your High Performance Pattern to identify what to do differently—how to work effectively to solve the problem. Patterns enable people to spot their off-pattern actions quickly. Then they can focus creative thinking on what to do *instead* to bring themselves back on pattern and get their activities back on track.

When people start new projects, their High Performance Patterns can help them decide how to move toward their goals most effectively, maximizing their opportunities for success. The steps in a pattern are like signposts: They point the way to the best possible line of action in any complex situation. Once a person has found an approach that fits his or her individual pattern, the person is far more confident of his or her capability for outstanding achievement.

When people are faced with choosing among different options—assignments, ways of doing something, prospects in a job search—their patterns help them identify in advance the alternative that fits best and offers the greatest potential for success. They can eliminate alternatives that will not produce high-performance results.

Managing Others

Patterns reveal how to manage individuals responsibly to get the best results that each can produce. Using patterns, a manager can work more easily with employees to find mutually acceptable ways for them to remain true to their individual patterns, satisfy the requirements of the corporate environment, and deliver outstanding results at the same time. Enduring success cannot come at the expense of the individual, the manager, or the organization.

As I noted in the Introduction, reality is messy. We all struggle to find a variation or application of a good idea that will produce a result superior to whatever we have been getting. The High Performance Pattern is a new and practical tool that simplifies and shortens that struggle. Patterns focus and facilitate the search for the uncompromising route to success.

How to Apply Patterns

Part II presents a series of case studies, each of which describes the application of a person's individual pattern to some real problem or opportunity. Although the process in each chapter is straightforward and detailed, I want to precede the case studies with an overview of our approach and its guiding principles.

Respect the Person's Uniqueness

The first principle is to treat the person's pattern with great respect. The pattern is the way in which this person works best, however bizarre it may seem and however tempted we may be to change or "improve" it. The most creative solutions, the ones that really work, emerge precisely because we refuse to jump to easy or conventional solutions that violate or ignore some step in the person's pattern. Because we are forced to respect the person's unique way of being successful, we must get creative about how to do the task.

Do a Point-by-Point Comparison

The process of applying a person's High Performance Pattern involves a point-by-point comparison of the steps in the pattern with the steps that he or she either is taking or is intending to take in the target situation. Then, for any step that the person executes weakly, he or she and anyone else involved focus on determining what to do differently—how to act more consistently with the pattern.

This process can be accomplished alone, and initially it often is. But I describe all the pattern-application processes in the book as an interaction between two people—typically me and the person I am helping. I do this for two reasons: first, to expose the thinking and decision-making process so that readers unfamiliar with patterns can grasp it. But I also have a deeper purpose. Numerous studies of human decision-making in natural settings demonstrate that people almost never make decisions alone. We may think through what we plan to do, but we virtually always talk it over with someone whom we trust: a spouse, a friend, an adviser, a teacher, a colleague, a boss.

The more important the decision, the more likely we are to talk it over with someone else. Good human decision making isn't done alone. For that reason, I always recommend interaction for planning and decision-making processes.

The prototypical interaction processes or protocols in this section should give you a good foundation for understanding the ensuing case studies. None of the cases conforms exactly to the protocols, but knowing the protocol will make following the process easier for you. In the protocols that follow, *M/C* stands for *Manager/Coach/Consultant/ Friend.* P stands for *Person.*

Type A Situation: Planning

In a Type A situation, the person is about to engage in a situation and wants it to go very very well.

Overall Task: Find the way for this person to approach the task that maximizes the chances of being highly successful.

M/C: *We know from your pattern that you do your best work when you [insert the action part of step 1 in the person's pattern]. Does the situation and what you are intending to do in it fit this step in your pattern?*

P answers *yes* or *no* and explains why or why not.

If the answer is *yes,* the M/C tests the answer against the wording of step 1 in the person's pattern, probing for whether it's actually true—does P's intended action fit the pattern step with real integrity? Then the M/C asks, *Is there anything you could do to fit the situation to step 1 even more?*

If the answer to the first question is *no,* M/C and P first identify and then agree on the aspect of the situation that doesn't fit. Then the M/C asks, *What steps might you take to adjust the situation so that it does fit? What would it take for the situation to really be right for you?* P makes suggestions. M/C adds ideas, then asks, *Wouldn't it fit your pattern even better if we could find some way that [insert the part of the step that isn't there] was present in the situation? Any way you can think of to make that happen?* P tries to come up with actions to increase the fit with step 1. M/C makes suggestions, but P has the absolute right to reject them. M/C writes down any suggestions or ideas that P agrees seem to have potential.

The M/C goes on to step 2 of the person's pattern.

M/C: We know that you do your best work when you [insert the action part of step 2 in the person's pattern]. How are you planning to do this? What are you thinking about doing that has real integrity with this step?

P explains what is planned and why it is or is not consistent with the step.

M/C tests the answer, pushing and probing for ways to enhance the fit between step 2 and what the person intends to do.

M/C writes down any improvements in the plan that P agrees seem to have potential.

M/C continues the process through each step of the person's pattern.

Keep the Person in Control

It is vital during this process to make sure that P—the person—stays in control. The manager, coach, consultant, or friend may be convinced that some suggestion is exactly what the person needs to do. If the person rejects the suggestion, the M/C will just have to come up with something else. The process is one of empowerment. Respect for the individual's way of working entails trusting that the rejection of a suggestion means that there is something wrong with the suggestion right now for this person.

As a rule, one or two steps prove difficult to get into place. When this happens, find a way for the person to act on pattern that is inspiring and energizing. Then the person is really ready to implement the plan. Sometimes you can identify the missing or weak step, but the necessary actions are either not obvious or they are problematic. At least you have identified the keystone step. I usually schedule a subsequent meeting near the time when the difficult step will approach in reality. I say, "Take the first three steps, and then let's talk again. By then, you will know more about the situation, and we'll probably be able to see how to activate step 4 of your pattern with integrity."

Type B Situation: Problem Solving

In a Type B situation, the person is part way into an assignment or activity, and it isn't going well. In some way, the person is off pattern.

Overall Task: Find where the person is off pattern and figure out a line of action that can correct it.

M/C: *If you were fully on pattern, the situation would be going better, so you must be off somewhere. Let's see if we can find where and figure out something you can do to correct the problem. We know from your pattern that you do your best work when you [insert the action part of step 1 in the person's pattern]. Have you done this? Does what you have already done fit this step in your pattern?*

P answers *yes* or *no* and explains why or why not.

If the answer is *yes,* the M/C tests the answer against the wording of step 1 in P's pattern, probing for whether it's accurate—has the person performed that pattern step with integrity? If the probing confirms that the person's action fits with step 1, go on to step 2.

If the answer is *no,* M/C and P first identify, then agree on the aspect of the situation that doesn't fit. Then M/C asks, *Is this where you are off pattern? What steps might you take to adjust the situation so that it does fit? What would it take to correct the situation so it really is right for you?* P makes suggestions. M/C adds ideas.

If the probing uncovers ways in which the person's actions don't exactly fit step 1, M/C feeds that back to the person, then asks, *Wouldn't it have fit your pattern even better if [insert the part of the step that isn't there] was present in the situation? Is that where you are off?*

If the person agrees with the assessment, M/C asks, *Any way you can think of to make that happen now?* P tries to come up with actions to correct the problem and thereby strengthen the fit with step 1. M/C does, too, and writes down any suggestions or ideas that seem to have potential.

The M/C goes on to step 2 of the person's pattern, looking to see if P is off on this step.

M/C: *We know that you do your best work when you [insert the action part of step 2 in the person's pattern]. Have you done this? Have you acted in a way that has real integrity with this step?*

P answers *yes* or *no* and explains why or why not.

M/C tests the answer, pushing and probing for ways to enhance the fit between step 2 and what the person has been doing.

The M/C continues the process through each step of the person's pattern, identifying all points where fit is off and corrective steps may be needed.

Earlier Steps Done Superficially or Not at All

When someone has trouble with a situation, he or she has usually left out some earlier step or performed it superficially instead of with real integrity. Let's say your pattern calls for obtaining clear authority from your boss when you work on a project. When we review a project that you're having trouble with, we discover that you sent a memo to the boss describing your intended actions and never got a reply. You didn't get a communication saying not to do it, but that's a far cry from clear authority. Your pattern shows that you need clear authorization to succeed. Because the authority to act was never clear, you have been proceeding tentatively, and when you encounter resistance, you don't feel empowered to countermand it. To resolve your problem, you need to return to the problem step of your pattern. Get a clear authorization from your boss, and the rest will be smooth sailing.

Type C Situation: Choosing

In a Type C situation, a person has several directions in which he or she can go and wants to choose the one that provides the highest likelihood of success.

Overall Task: Find the option that best fits the person's pattern.

For this prototype, although any example involving choice would work, let's assume that someone is looking for a new assignment within a large company.

M/C: As I understand it, your company has offered you three options for reassignment. Tell me a little bit about each of them.

P describes each of the three positions.

M/C: We know you'll be most likely to succeed if you can do your next job in a way that fits you. Let's look at each step of your pattern and discuss which of the three options seems to fit it best.

P agrees.

M/C: What do you think? Does option A fit step 1 of your pattern? Option B? Option C?

P responds, while M/C probes.

M/C: *Which one fits step 1 best?*

P responds. Together they identify the one that fits best initially, the one that looks like it would fit best in the long run, and what P might be able to negotiate going in that would make each option fit even better.

The M/C writes down all specific good ideas.

M/C: *Let's go on to step 2. Which option fits it best?*

Together they continue to look at each step until the preferred option emerges. Many times, examination reveals that further negotiations with the different options are indicated. These negotiations may cause one option to improve.

Let the Person Make the Final Choice

Type C is a variation on Type A, which focuses on planning. It involves mapping the pattern onto each of several options that a person has in order to see which fits best. I've described it separately in order to illustrate some nuances.

Once an option has been identified and the pattern has been compared with the assignment description and the known facts, there are always a number of areas in which the new assignment doesn't fit. We are very careful to let the person decide whether to take the assignment. We believe in the empowerment that patterns give people to make their own choices. Some choose situations that fit their patterns well going in. Others choose situations that don't fit, because they relish the task of adjusting them and because they bet that their unique way of succeeding will prove a competitive advantage.

In either case, we go through the planning process to identify areas of fit and lack of fit with each opportunity. We then strongly recommend that a person negotiate in advance about the areas that don't fit. You have much more leverage before you take the assignment than you do after. Your pattern identifies precisely what is missing or what will throw you off pattern. Attempting to correct things in advance will elicit the kind of reaction that you are likely to receive after you are in the job. Forewarned is forearmed.

The Case Examples

The cases that follow in the next ten chapters show this process over and over, repeated with different individuals, patterns, situations, and goals. Each time, there is a way of connecting the person's best way of working with the situation that doesn't violate or compromise either. Do patterns work? You be the judge.

- Chapter 5 shows Rebecca Allen using the pattern derived in Chapter 2 to plan a way to reenergize an ongoing assigned task, the budgeting process, that she had already done fifteen times and that she was very tired of.

- Chapter 6 returns to Nick Rostov as he uses his pattern to figure out why he can't get the division heads to agree on a common process and what he has to do to secure agreement.

- Chapter 7 follows manager Bob Anderson as he uses his pattern to determine why a critical project in his division isn't getting anywhere, what mistakes he made in launching it, and how to correct the problem.

- Chapter 8 describes how Regina Gold used her pattern to sift job openings for which she was qualified, pick the one that fit her best, and then plan how to conduct herself so she would be on pattern in the job interview and get the job.

- Chapter 9 describes how a busy executive, Jack Grand, used his pattern to plan a family vacation so that he would actually take it, regardless of the crises or demands that his job might present.

- Chapter 10 shows how service manager Mike Draker used his pattern to figure out how he could approach a sales job in a way that would work for him, since it was the only job available.

- Chapter 11 follows insurance salesman Joe Porter's process of using his pattern to leap from worst to second-best salesperson in an office of forty agents by staying true to his pattern, not by trying to imitate what successful colleagues were doing.

- Chapter 12 describes how vice president Marsha Kemp used her pattern to think through the best way of turning around a dead operation and the surprises she found when she did it in a way that fit her.

- Chapter 13 illustrates how executive Tomas Vargas used his pattern to find a way to be true to his personal values of deep concern for others while executing a corporate decision that required him to fire many employees.

- Chapter 14 illustrates the benefits of using a pattern, even if the line of action doesn't work, by following how financial planner Patricia Rosenberg attempted to correct problems her office landlord was ignoring and that were affecting her business, and finally moved her offices when she couldn't resolve the dispute.

5

Revitalizing a Task You Are Stuck with and Sick Of

THE CASE OF MANAGING A COMPANY BUDGETING PROCESS

As we began to apply Rebecca Allen's High Performance Pattern, she was feeling very tired of her job. She told me, "I've been a budget analyst coordinating the preparation of a budget in some large organization for more than fifteen years. I'm ready for a change."

Looking back over her ten years at Rocky Mountain Water, Rebecca realized that she had improved the budgeting process significantly. Ten years earlier, each department manager simply sent in his requests and justifications. Both format and justification were inconsistent from one department to another, a fact that made it very difficult to compare costs and justifications across departments and set organizational priorities.

Rebecca had systematized the budgeting process over time. Under her system, departments received guidance for determining their budgets whenever possible. She also initiated standard formats and established principles of comparison for proposals. She made the budgeting process participatory. Separate departments cooperated to develop their individual budgets. Rebecca was proud that, under her leadership, all departments and divisions collaborated in the final cutting process to meet the board's overall budgetary limits. She played a dual role in all this, working with departments to develop justifications for their requests and serving on the decision-making group that approved or disapproved these requests. Rebecca was justifiably proud that she had no particular problem changing hats. She felt that departments and top decision makers alike trusted her.

In spite of all these positives, further probing revealed that the budget process would be more difficult than usual this year. The past year had seen huge turnover in top management. Rebecca's boss, who headed engineering, plus the general manager and several of his senior executives had all left. The new general manager was reorganizing the company on a massive scale. No one knew yet what direction the completed reorganization would take. Consequently, morale was at an all-time low.

No one knew yet to whom they would be reporting. This included Rebecca. Apparently, the engineering department was to be eliminated as a separate entity. With her new boss and the new general manager, Rebecca was having difficulty establishing the rapport and influence that she had enjoyed with the old ones. Both new superiors were only a year into the job, and both were still finding out whom in the organization they felt comfortable trusting. Although Rebecca understood this dynamic, she was chafing under her lack of solid authority and influence—qualities that she needed if she was to fulfill her responsibilities.

Rebecca's Thoughts About What Was Wrong in the Organization

Rebecca had the insight that, with everything in flux, the company responded only to a crisis. In a crisis, everyone pulled together, exerting enormous energy to do whatever it took to rectify the situation. It always worked—they did a great job.

Although this capacity to come through in a crisis is a remarkably positive thing in normal times, in the current context it was a drawback. Rising to meet a crisis was becoming the organizational norm. Nothing got done unless it was done that way. Everyone was working long hours. Everyone was worn out. To make matters worse, the company didn't recognize or reward their efforts. Because crisis intervention was rapidly becoming standard operating procedure, the group was simply expected to marshal its forces in that extraordinary way again and again.

In this climate, departments perceived the budgeting process as one more impossible burden. Rebecca felt that the organization would find the time to complete the budget but in a way that would only perpetuate the debilitating crisis mentality.

What Rebecca Would Have Done If She Hadn't Known Her Pattern

Rebecca felt that, if she had not known her pattern, the contextual instability and her current lack of upward influence would have led her to push the budget process through by sheer personal force of will. She was a very skilled facilitator. She was certain she had the credibility and relationships with lower-level people that she needed to get the job done. She was also convinced that this would not have been personally satisfying. It would certainly have been a grind-it-out, not a high-performance, experience!

A recent outside commitment reflected Rebecca's current sense of hopelessness about her immediate future: To satisfy her need to expand her horizons and make a difference, she had just joined the steering committee for the huge national conference of her favorite professional association.

How Rebecca's Pattern Helped Uncover an Alternative

Working only from Rebecca's High Performance Pattern, one item at a time, we explored how she might approach the budgeting process in a way that fit her best way of working. We let the pattern suggest fresh ways of looking at the activity and then tested them for feasibility. (Rebecca's entire pattern appeared on page 42.)

We started, of course, with the first step:

1. I perceive an opportunity to improve or upgrade a complex process involving overlapping issues and multiple people that is creeping along, causing a lot of gridlock.

It was immediately obvious in light of step 1 that the budgeting process had potential for being a high-performance experience for Rebecca. She consistently did her best work when upgrading some complex process that was creeping along. However, if she persisted in her established approach, this year's budget process would merely continue to creep along. How could she improve or upgrade it amid the current organizational upheaval? If we could find that way, the first factor in getting her to her high-performance mode would kick in.

We cast about for a way to think about and then carry out the budgeting process that would be a marked improvement or upgrade. Although Rebecca was also considering changing jobs, that wouldn't happen immediately. She needed a short-term solution. If we could make the approach fit her pattern, she wouldn't have to grind her way through this process one more time. She would have a shot at seeing it go better than expected.

It emerged in the course of our discussions that a budgeting process, done well, could be a stabilizing force in a time of rapid change. Setting a budget was familiar. It reassured people that they would have jobs, even if they weren't exactly sure what the reporting structure would be. It reassured people that certain work would proceed, even if the exact assignments weren't clear. And in the absence of articulated policy directions, a well-structured budget with alternatives could force the organization to make needed decisions. Rebecca's success in stabilizing the organization during this trying time would vastly benefit her new boss and the new general manager, thereby increasing her influence and credibility with higher-ups. Rebecca liked the idea immensely.

Working through step 1 gave us our theme for the way in which Rebecca could turn budgeting into a high-performance experience: *Cast the budgeting process as a stabilizing force in this trying time of change.* Next, we needed to make sure that we tied in the remaining items of her pattern to create her complete plan of action.

2. I see a way to improve the relationships among the people involved (including myself) by doing it.

Rebecca had no doubt that, in turning the budgetary process away from the prevailing crisis orientation, she would generate great gratitude among those in the organization, particularly those in the engineering division. People would feel that they had some influence over the organization's ultimate shape, even while its specific internal structure was still in flux.

I pushed her hard about what she could actually do to make the process less crisis oriented. Somewhat to my surprise, she immediately ticked off a list of specifics. She decided she could greatly simplify the process by centralizing the formatting of numbers so that each department manager did not have to make sure that every number was in the right box. This would allow department managers to concentrate on the programmatic and financial justifications for their requests. Managers would love relief from detailed bean counting.

Rebecca listed several other possibilities. She could provide even more guidelines and parameters. By pooling certain items and the money for them, she could limit the number of requests requiring justification or explanation. For example, each department needing only one or two more personal computers wouldn't be burdened with individual justifications. As Rebecca rattled off a string of very specific modifications that could give the budgeting process a highly positive role in helping the organization cope with imminent change, she got excited. We turned to the next step in her pattern to see what it would add to the developing plan.

> 3. I get myself into a position to improve something by being asked to do it or by getting it assigned to me and agreeing to take it on.

This step was slightly more problematic. Rebecca knew she could accomplish it within the engineering division. At first, she considered doing only that—after all, engineering was 40 percent of the overall budget and more than 75 percent of the capital budget. But I pushed her to shun the easy way out. How could she get assigned to do the job for the entire organization?

We realized that in order to carry out her plan companywide, she would have to make the business case for it to the new general manager. We talked about some possible approaches. She could explain to him that his understandably time-consuming massive restructuring was having fallout in terms of low morale. She could then demonstrate how her simplification of the budgetary process would remove many such negative side effects well before his reorganization was firmly established. The more we talked, the more Rebecca felt convinced both that she could present the budgeting process in this unusual way and that it would really pay off.

Rebecca acknowledged that she had never considered positioning the budgeting process in this way nor of using it to get herself assigned to the work and to obtain the authority that she needed to make the plan work. It all made very good sense. But, if her pattern had not suggested this solution, it would never have occurred to her. And the risk was minimal. The the worst the general manager could do was say no.

Nonetheless, Rebecca decided to make the business case to her division manager first. That would help her practice her presentation. If her manager agreed, she could direct the process within her own division in a way that exemplified her plan for the whole organization. With that foundation, she would look for an opportunity to convince the general manager.

> **4. I interview the others involved to describe what I have in mind and to determine their ideas, agendas, and objectives, using my interpersonal skills to gain their trust and cooperation.**

It was easy to see how to build this step in. Rebecca would meet with the budget analysts responsible for various departments and involve them in her thinking. She would also include key department managers. She was sure they would all add many ideas for giving the budgetary process a stabilizing function and for ultimately formulating her proposal so the general manager would buy it. And she was sure they would all be enthusiastic.

> **5. I pull my thoughts together into a draft plan and reach agreement with the others on the objective, the plan, and what the results will look like.**

This step suggested that, after initial discussion with the budget analysts and department managers, Rebecca should draft her proposal. She should return the draft to them for refinements before eliciting their final approval. She saw no problem here.

> **6. I lay out my conditions to do the task and get agreement from the powers-that-be for the independent authority and resources that I need. I offer in return to get it done and to have regular, straight communication.**

This was the critical step. Rebecca would have to take the proposal first to her division manager and then to the general manager, getting agreement and authorization from each of them before proceeding. Rebecca's weak spot was in the second sentence of the step. She realized that *she often did not take time to make regular progress reports to top people.* We flagged the step as crucial to the outcome of her plan. We decided to return later to examine why she often omitted this step, which was key to building the trust needed for the influence that she wanted. We resolved to plan ways of making sure that she performed the step this time.

> 7. I take on some of the actual work myself and ensure that others understand their tasks and roles by checking in with key people (individually and collectively) to keep information flowing.

I asked Rebecca to identify the pieces of this project that she would keep for herself. She answered without hesitation that she would facilitate the decision-making process from the wish list stage onward, particularly the meetings with higher-ups in which priorities would be set and the budget approved.

> 8. I establish one other key person as a sounding board with whom I can review and brainstorm any issue and overall progress.

Rebecca told me that this had always been the most important step for her—she fights to preserve it in everything she does. Without a person to act as sounding board, things do not go well for her. I asked her to list people by name who could serve in this key capacity. After Rebecca named two department analysts with whom she had great rapport and another person in the corporate budget office, we felt that we had incorporated this step into the evolving plan.

> 9. I go with my gut feelings whenever I have to reassess priorities, plans, or work with others to make mid-course changes or other major decisions.

Because the remaining items on Rebecca's pattern involved how to act once the budgeting process was really under way, it was harder to plan for them in detail. Nevertheless, I asked whether anything in this step would serve as a critical reminder to her. She named the gut feelings in decision making as a good flag. When something interfered with the smooth running of her projects, she tended, she said, to "think too much." She could easily foresee that another crisis would arise while she was trying to implement a stabilizing budgetary process. At that juncture, she would have to rely on her gut feelings to maintain the project and not let it be dropped.

10. I keep balance in my life by maintaining several simultaneous activities and shift from one to another for renewal and perspective.

This step posed no problem. Rebecca had several other responsibilities. I pointed out that, since it was in her pattern, it was *important* for her not to let the budgeting process become too all-consuming. She did her best work only when she had several stimulating things going on simultaneously. She agreed.

11. I stay with the project until the identified end objective is evident or the phase has run its course.

Obviously, Rebecca would do this if she could. The key, she felt, was to resist being sidetracked by other demands on her time. She felt that her handling of step 6—the "contracting" step—would determine how well she could avoid getting swept off-course. She needed to get agreement up front that higher-ups would not pull her off the project.

12. I take time to provide a transition for those who will maintain the process and implement the outcome.

Rebecca realized that this step in her pattern required her to relinquish the project to someone else for maintenance. She had already told me that she was tired of handling budgets, so this step suggested that she should identify someone who would take on the budgeting process after the current year. She promised to think about possible successors. Her assistant was the logical choice, but Rebecca wanted to mull it over. She also recognized her lack of control over this particular step—a dilemma for someone with a pattern like hers. If the organization insisted on assigning the budget process to her, Rebecca would not be able to fulfill the requirements of her pattern in this instance.

13. I find I've been incorporated into and become an acknowledged part of the success of someone else, receiving thanks and recognition for my good work.

When Rebecca read this step, she realized that this element was missing from her job. She wasn't getting much thanks or recognition. I asked her what would be the right kind of reward. She felt she needed at least a public thank you. A merit pay bonus, a salary increase, and serious consideration for a newly opened corporate budget management position would be even better. Rebecca had already decided to apply for the new position, but she didn't feel that she would be considered a serious candidate.

Rebecca connected this step with step 6 in her pattern. To gain recognition and consideration for promotion, she would need to be rigorous about reporting back, with results in hand, to the division manager and ultimately to the general manager throughout the process. She could also specify these forms of recognition as a precondition for taking the project on.

14. I assess, over time, the actual value of what I did, observe the applications, and consider how to do better the next time.

This step was a regular part of nearly everything that Rebecca did. Ironically, in all the recent organizational turmoil, she hadn't yet completed a postmortem on the previous year's budget process. Putting the current proposal together would serve that purpose. The lasting evidence of the value of her present plan would be that her simplified budgeting format was used in the years to come.

Some Reflections on the Process

Using her pattern, Rebecca needed less than two hours for the entire planning process just described. She started the process feeling very tired and stressed about having to do the budget again. By the end of our session, she was truly excited, energized, and looking forward to the challenge. She had devised a way to meet her personal needs and those of the corporation. Now she just needed to pull it off.

Would Rebecca have come up with this idea without her pattern? She is convinced that she would not have. Even so, she was already aware of most elements in her plan: the dual need for some stabilizing activity and for simplification of the budgeting process to reduce departmental burdens. But only connecting the project with her personal High Performance Pattern could suggest a way of knitting these pieces together and selling it to the corporation as the right thing to do.

Contrary to general expectations, we find that most organizations have plenty of room for creative methodologies. But how a proposal is positioned can make all the difference in the world to its acceptance. Without some process to stimulate out-of-the-box thinking, people often see no alternative to plodding through in the way they've always done. At best, they half-formulate a path, omitting major steps toward a successful outcome.

Often the only way in which good ideas can be packaged so they actually work is to connect them with some person's driving energy. Rebecca describes this function of patterns as putting that personal force into a form that can be applied to decision making in real situations. Patterns activate driving energy.

6

Finding a Winning Strategy in a Corporate Power Struggle

THE CASE OF THE UNCOOPERATIVE DIVISION HEADS

Chapter 5 illustrated one of the three principal uses of High Performance Patterns: planning an activity so that it fits the doer and he or she can therefore do it well. This chapter illustrates another use: problem solving. Nick Rostov's story shows how a person's pattern can be used to assess why some project is not going well and determine what can be done differently to get the person and the activity back on track.

This case also shows how one individual's pattern can often provide the clue to what is wrong in a problem involving many other people, even when their High Performance Patterns are not known. You don't need to know each participant's pattern or do complex analyses of all the interacting forces to resolve a complex problem. Having just one person take responsibility and act with integrity can do wonders to sort out a politically complicated and confusing situation. Nick's case is one of many that I could have chosen to illustrate this point.

When we first found Nick's pattern, he was human resources director at a large electronics firm. He had been working on a particular issue for months without success. Although his approaches should have worked, none had. Nick was frustrated and at a loss. Why didn't his solutions work? When Nick and I used his pattern to assess his behavior in the situation at hand, we discovered that he was off pattern in one significant way. Taking action to get himself back on track, Nick was soon able to resolve the problem. Moreover, although his approach seemed to be confrontational, he behaved responsibly—forcing the others involved to act responsibly, too. Nick's individual courage to act with integrity benefited everyone concerned.

Nick's Data-Reporting Dilemma

Human resources was responsible for producing a monthly report on the company's employment status by department—people hired, people who left, overall salary costs. It seemed like a simple task. But month after month, it took four or five days to produce the report. And every month, all the division heads attacked the report as inaccurate or misleading. Nick wanted to get the issue resolved once and for all—to reduce the effort to half a day per month, the amount of time that he thought reasonable.

What Nick Thought Was Wrong and
What He Had Been Doing to Correct It

Nick had selected a standard way of reporting head count data from each department that fit the company's various employment categories. He had investigated a variety of formats before making a final selection. His major concern was that everyone use a consistent standard for data to be comparable across divisions and months.

The format that Nick had selected was a very good one for his purposes. But much to his surprise, the division heads all fought the reporting standard he proposed. They all claimed that special conditions in their own division meant that the results of consistent formulas would be misleading. Each division insisted on reporting its data in a different way, and each argued that its way was best.

Nick had approached the problem by meeting individually and collectively with division heads. He had indicated that he was willing to adopt a different standard if it proved better, since establishing a single consistent standard was the top priority. He had assumed that he could engage the division heads in a process of give-and-take discussion until they all agreed on a single reporting system, at least for an initial trial.

Nick's efforts to achieve consensus failed. Every month, the division heads changed their minds about what they wanted him to do. Every month, he came back with a new way of collecting and reporting the data, only to have them reject his new proposal. For months he had been reduced to taking incompatible data from each division and transforming it himself to conform to some standard. This not only took a lot of time, it also opened Nick to attack when the report summary was released.

Point-by-Point Comparison

To help Nick figure out what was wrong and what he could do about it, we compared his High Performance Pattern, point by point, with what he was currently doing to solve the report problem. Our starting assumption was that, if Nick were on pattern, he would not have the problem, or at least he would not be frustrated by it. He would either correct it or decide that it wasn't worth the effort. Our task was to find out where Nick was off pattern and what his pattern suggested that he should do to correct it.

We worked through each step until we saw where he had derailed. (Nick's entire pattern appeared on page 55.)

> 1. I get engaged with an activity I have not done before that gives me a chance to show how well I can do, and I want to do it well.

Nick thought about it and definitely agreed that producing the report fit this step of his pattern. He hadn't done it before. It wasn't trivial. The report was going to be highly visible, so it would give him a chance to show what he could do. He definitely wanted to do it well, even if his initial focus was on reducing the amount of time that it took his staff to produce the report.

To maximize the fit with step 1, I pushed Nick to come up with the most powerful framework that he could for grasping the importance of the activity. As we talked, Nick realized that the opposition from the division heads made this an opportunity to show that he could provide leadership in a difficult situation. This last insight intrigued Nick. His frustration had been high because he had been thinking merely of "getting this damned little report out of my hair." He hadn't recognized the big-picture implications. Once he saw the report in the context of getting the division heads to work together, he got very excited.

2. I recognize that "tests" are an inherent part of the activity and that ultimately what I do will be put to a significant test that I'm not sure I can pull off.

As his experience had shown, Nick's report was going to be subjected to very severe "tests" by the division heads, not to mention the ultimate test of its value to corporate officers. The division heads were going to take every opportunity to criticize the report. Nick realized as we talked that, without the resistance that made him unsure he could pull it off, the situation would not have high-performance potential for him. The fact that he had run into so much active opposition made the assignment very much on pattern for him. It was certainly true that at this point Nick wasn't sure he could pull it off.

3. I start it, find that getting good at it intrigues me, and get completely drawn into it.

The assignment had intrigued Nick from the beginning. Just having to research and select the best reporting format made it interesting as business analysis. By the time I started working with him, months of frustration with the division heads had made Nick even more intrigued. He wanted the problem solved, but he was also driven to understand what was going on. He knew that the format he proposed was solid, so the constant opposition only piqued him. Nick was definitely on pattern with step 3.

4. I identify every aspect of the activity and work on mastering them one at a time until I understand how to exploit their possibilities fully.

Nick had begun by mastering every aspect of producing the report. There were many possible formats. Each had certain things to recommend it, and there were many different ways to define *employment*. He had studied all the options, determined how to make the report valuable to executives, and recommended the best format. Now that he had run into such opposition, Nick realized that there were even more factors to master, and he definitely wanted to get on top of them.

Because he had missed some of these dynamics, Nick was somewhat off pattern here but only in a way common to any activity. Once a person acts, the external world reacts in unpredictable ways. I resisted speculating on the reasons that division heads had for opposing Nick's report. High Performance Patterns work for people over and over in their lives. If we could just find a way for Nick to stay true to his pattern, it would work for him again. I wanted us to look at the whole pattern. I suspected that there was some other, less obvious way in which Nick was not being true to his pattern. If he corrected that problem, the seemingly political opposition would dissolve. Even so, we knew that we needed to talk more about this. We flagged it and went on.

> 5. I weave all the strands together into the best model I can create for the requirements of the situation.

Nick had performed this step for the report. He was convinced that, given the requirements of the situation, he had recommended the best way of reporting the figures. Now that he had encountered opposition, he needed to decide how committed he was to his model. As I tested his conviction, Nick reasserted that he was sure he had the best model, although there were other alternatives. I suggested that, given his pattern, *the most important thing was for him to be committed to his model and stay committed to it.* He could adjust it if he found a better one but not just for political reasons. His pattern suggested that he worked best if he developed the best model he could and tested it. I wanted him to stay true to his pattern.

> 6. I recognize there is an unknown or uncontrollable element that adds uncertainty to the outcome and heightens my concentration.

There certainly was an unknown and apparently uncontrollable element adding uncertainty: the absence of agreement among division heads and the fact that they constantly changed their minds about what they wanted. The behavior of the division heads was causing Nick to pay a lot more attention to the issue. He was on pattern here.

7. I pilot test and refine the model until it is elegant and polished.

Nick had polished his model to perfection. Every time there had been some objection to the report for a particular month, he had considered the report and corrected it if he could or if he thought the objection made sense. He felt now that he could answer every possible objection to the way he was proposing to handle reporting the figures. Yet the opposition remained. The question was, What to do about it? Again, Nick was on pattern.

As long as we considered only the way in which Nick produced the report, he was on pattern through the first seven steps: It was a new activity he wanted to do well; he was being tested on it; it was drawing him in, and he was mastering every aspect of it; he had created the best model he could; and in the face of the uncertainty he had polished the model to perfection. To this point we could find nothing to indicate that he was out of synch with what worked best for him. So why wasn't it going better? The assignment seemed to fit him perfectly, even in that the opposition had intensified his concentration. All his high-performance stories had involved considerable opposition.

It was at step 8 of Nick's pattern that we found the key insight.

8. I give the model the ultimate test, running it just as planned, and it works fabulously, building to an incredible crescendo.

Clearly, Nick was not giving his own model the ultimate test. Instead of insisting that his model be followed until experience proved it right or wrong, he was approaching division heads almost tentatively, indicating up front a willingness to compromise on his model. Far from compromising, the division heads had effectively been preventing Nick from putting any kind of standard model to the test.

Someone other than Nick, someone whose High Performance Pattern involved political maneuvering and working out quid pro quo agreements with individual division heads, would have taken a quite different tack. That person's approach would have worked if he or she had stayed true to that way of being successful. But Nick's way of being successful was to refine a model and then test it. He had to make that happen here.

Once Nick saw how he had gone off pattern by not insisting that his own model be tested, he saw clearly what he needed to do. Rather than speculating on why the division heads were not willing to have a standard model (or were trying to prevent him from putting one in place), he needed to get on with it. He also saw the kind of downward spiral that can start once a person gets off pattern. He had been blaming himself. He had assumed there was something wrong with his interpersonal or communication skills. The division heads were older than he, they had considerably more power, and he had been blaming his own lack of experience. Being off pattern is a quick route to loss of confidence.

At this point, Nick realized that the most important thing for him to do was to test the model. He was quite willing to sink or swim based on the results, which he knew would be good. He also decided to accept the fact that he would never resolve his dilemma working with division heads and submitting to their decisions. He had tried. He had much less status and power than they did, and he couldn't compel them to agree. He would have to go over their heads, present his model to their boss or their boss's boss, answer all the objections that they would raise, and have them order the division heads to comply with his format.

Nick also knew, of course, that this was a decision point in his relationship with division heads. He could continue to grind out the report each month and deal with their obstructive behaviors without confronting them, or he could force the issue to resolution and pay whatever short-term price was required to get it settled to his satisfaction. By this time also, Nick had been through so many variations in reporting formats that he could explain exactly what was needed and exactly what was lost by the absence of standardization. He felt sure that he could win the case higher up.

When we looked at the last two items of his pattern, Nick felt comfortable about his plan:

9. I receive clear, positive test results that show how well I've done.

10. I feel satisfied that I have proven my ability and deserve to play at the new level of accomplishment.

Approval would be the clear, positive result he sought. Even more, once his report started to improve decision making, it would be another clear, positive result. Furthermore, he would feel he deserved to play in the same league with the division heads, rather than be treated as their lackey. It was an essential reward, something that made the effort worthwhile.

Using his pattern bolstered Nick's confidence. He felt he knew exactly what the right course was for him to be successful. So he had the courage to act. He did in fact elevate the dispute above the division heads. He carefully prepared the arguments in favor of his model, demonstrating that having a standard reporting system was critical. And he prepared arguments that showed the kinds of comparisons that his model would make possible and how they would be valuable at the vice presidential level. Then he took the problem upstairs.

Nick had to go two levels up to reach an executive vice president to whom all the division heads reported. Within a matter of weeks, he had a favorable decision. His model was chosen as the way in which head count would be reported.

Perhaps Nick's biggest lesson came after he won and had to face the response of the division heads. They were delighted. After fighting for years, they now had accurate comparative data across divisions, which they found very useful in their own planning and management. Far from having the punitive uses that they feared, the data comparisons proved to be very beneficial to all divisions. They simply had not been able to agree on it by themselves. It had taken someone who was willing to kick the issue upstairs. And Nick's department went from spending four or five days a month on the report to half a day of one clerk's time.

After the fact, Nick told me what he thought had been going on politically. Each division head wanted to report the data in the way that made his or her management decisions about head count and deployment of personnel seem the most rational and defensible. Nick had been caught in the middle of a political power struggle among them. Adaptation of a standard reporting procedure made it possible to calculate ratios comparing head count and dollars spent on salaries for operations in different parts of the company. Without a standard model, no such comparisons could be made. Since division heads were under constant pressure to reduce head count, they wanted to be able to conceal what they were doing from their superiors and leave them no excuse for interfering with the way they ran their divisions. They thought that it was in their individual and collective self-interest not to have a standard report.

When Nick acted just to be true to himself in the situation, it gave other people room to get out of their closed-loop thinking.

What Nick's Use of His Pattern Added to Resolving the Data-Reporting Dilemma

Would Nick eventually have resolved his data-reporting dilemma in this way if he had not known his pattern?

Nick doesn't think so. His pattern showed Nick that testing his model was what he really needed to do. He knew that his model would work well, and that helped him to take responsibility for his own moves towards success. Nick's High Performance Pattern helped give him the confidence and courage that he needed to take on the division heads.

We find that people can accomplish an astonishing amount of good for their companies if they take their High Performance Patterns seriously and act with integrity to be true to them. So many situations get out of control because no one is willing to take responsibility for getting results. High Performance Patterns help people gain the insights and confidence that they need to act in ways they know can be successful. In this, they help everyone else.

7

Getting a Critical Project Back on Track

THE CASE OF TAKING WHO'S AVAILABLE INSTEAD OF WHO'S RIGHT FOR THE JOB

As I move into relating other cases showing how High Performance Patterns can be used, you need to keep in mind that in every example the pattern was derived from three or more individual high-performance stories, just as it was for Rebecca and Nick. In every case, we analyzed the stories carefully. The resulting pattern was empirically determined. Like it or not, the pattern represents how each person actually does his or her best work, so the approach in every example is to find a way of accomplishing the particular objective that is consistent with the person's pattern and that works within the policies and constraints of the current situation. All the cases that I am about to review are real. To maintain confidentiality, I have changed the names and enough of the significant facts to disguise the person and the company.

This chapter examines the case of Bob, an executive in a large consumer products distribution company. At the time when I worked with him, one of his most critical improvement projects was stalled. He thought he needed to act in a particular way to improve the performance of one of his subordinates who was in charge of it, but his way of acting seemed to be getting nowhere. When Bob's pattern showed what was really wrong—that he had gone off track and how—he decided to do something quite different.

The Stalled Critical Project

Bob Anderson runs the warehousing and distribution systems for a $4 billion consumer products manufacturing and distribution company. He is vice president and division manager of the company, which has operations nationwide and a reputation for efficiency. Bob has been a company leader in cutting operating expenses, reducing his division's expenses by 7 to 10 percent a year over the past seven years. In this way, he has kept his division's expenses flat in inflated dollars and greatly increased the company's profit margins.

Bob has been with the company more than twenty years if we include the ten years when what is now his division was an independent business. He has more than 4,000 employees and enjoys a good reputation among those whom he manages. Bob has effective interpersonal skills, and he is a high performer.

Over the past three years, Bob had sought and finally won permission to implement a vastly different budgeting system for the company, one that he thought would be key in continuing his cost-cutting successes. In the simplest terms, he wanted a way to figure out budgets for the coming year not in terms of the previous year's budget but in terms of the best that could theoretically be achieved for each division.

As Bob put it, "If the division had a profit margin of 10 in some warehouse in the preceding year, they typically try for 11 the next year. But what if 20 was possible? Thinking in terms of 20 rather than 11 would increase efficiency greatly." Bob called the new system he wanted to implement *base report budgeting*. He saw links between it and the Japanese system of zero manufacturing defects.

Although Bob was the principal proponent of implementing the new base report cost-cutting accounting system throughout the entire company, he found that preliminary development of the system was stalled in his own department.

"On my part, there is a lot of frustration about this project," Bob explained. "After six months, we have produced nothing but talk. We don't have any products or sample procedures, and there's no consensus on what to do or how to do it. I really think I know what should be done, and I've articulated that. But we just haven't moved nearly as well as I'd like to."

High Performance Pattern
for Bob Anderson

1. I take on a major undertaking that has some very tricky aspects to it but that will pay off in long-range, self-sustaining benefits.

2. I strongly believe that the choice of what to do is the right thing to do; I would not be happy doing anything less.

3. I immediately move into action once the decision to proceed has been made, not letting protocol stand in the way of the timing required by the situation.

4. I draw on my past experience to bring in outstanding people to manage the undertaking—people who will personalize it and take the extra step to make it happen.

5. I continually research and plan, research and plan, staying in close touch with all levels of the people involved and the mood of the situation, working to foresee all the problems that could come up, and preparing to meet them.

6. I insist, even to the point of obstinacy, not just on doing it right but on doing it perfectly.

7. I personally do whatever is necessary to keep the undertaking going strong, including sitting in the hotseat and taking whatever criticism is directed at me.

8. I make sure that the people involved at all levels know how much I value and care about them by telling them so and by showing a great deal of support in a temperate way.

9. I succeed in pulling the whole thing off and leaving behind a positive, proactive, and self-sustaining operation.

10. I am deeply satisfied with how successful the undertaking has been and by how well everyone has been served.

Bob's Pattern Shows How He Is off Pattern
and How He Can Get Back on Track

To see how Bob could put the standard report project back on track, I used his High Performance Pattern as a guide. Step by step, I had Bob look at his own actions in developing the project thus far, asking whether he had followed with integrity each of the steps that his High Performance Pattern suggested. Because Bob's pattern had brought him success in the past, it was reasonable to expect that following the steps of the pattern would bring him success now.

Once Bob had identified the steps in the pattern that he had not followed—the places where he was off pattern—he quickly understood how to reassign personnel and redirect the base report project so that it would work.

The best way to apply a High Performance Pattern in a problem situation is to treat each step of the pattern as if it were a question about the situation that can be answered yes or no. If the answer is a true yes, you can go on to the next step. If it is no, you need to decide what the individual needs to do in this particular situation to make the answer yes. To highlight this concept, I have turned the first four steps of Bob's pattern into questions, or what we call checklist format.

The process, of course, was identical to the process with Nick: We compared his pattern with what he had actually done, probed to be sure that he had performed with integrity the steps that appeared to match his pattern, and explored alternatives if he appeared to be off pattern. The answers were quite revealing and insightful both to Bob and to me, particularly when we reached step 4 of Bob's pattern.

1. Is this project a major undertaking that, while tricky, will ultimately have long-range, self-sustaining benefits?

I knew from Bob's pattern that he did his best work when he was involved in a major undertaking that had some tricky aspects and some long-range benefits. Was this true of the base report project? Bob assured me that he was right on target in this step: "I am proposing a way of measuring costs with computer programs and doing it very differently than it has been done in the past," he said. "Essentially, I'm asking that budgets be set against an optimum standard rather than against last year's budget results. Not many people in the company think this is worth doing, but I think it's critical if the company wants to improve cost controls over the next ten years."

From my point of view, Bob was not off pattern on this step. The problem must lie somewhere else.

2. Do you believe that this choice of what to do is the right thing to do? Would you not be happy doing anything less?

I recognized that Bob was most effective when he believed strongly that he was advocating the right thing to do. Bob is the driving force behind the standard report, but does he believe that it is the right choice? I probed to find out. "Is it really true," I asked, "that you won't be happy if you have to settle for something less?"

"I am strongly behind the base report project as the right thing to do," Bob replied. "I really believe that if we don't do this, we'll be stuck, unable to continue to find creative ways of cutting costs further."

Bob and I agreed that he wasn't off pattern here. As he put it after thinking about it carefully, "Bingo! This item fits to a tee!"

3. Did you immediately move into action once the decision to proceed had been made, not letting protocol stand in the way of the timing required by the situation?

Since Bob does his best when he doesn't let rules or formalities stand in his way, I asked if he saw a problem with this step. Had he moved immediately into action?

Bob's answer was yes. Although he had waited several years to start on the project, he had moved very quickly once the opportunity was there. Bob did not seem to be off pattern here either, so we kept on looking.

4. Did you draw on your past experience to bring in outstanding people to manage the undertaking—people who will personalize it and take the extra step to make it happen?

Bob's pattern told me that he needed to have chosen an outstanding person to manage his undertaking, one who would work extra hard to bring it to success. Does Patrick Davis, the employee whom he selected, fit the bill? Here, Bob's answers began to indicate some deviation from the way in which he had acted in his high-performance examples.

"Well, I have been more patient than usual," Bob said carefully, noticing his own demeanor as he spoke. "Patrick Davis is the only resource person working for me to drive this program, and I have really let him find his own way on it. Frankly, I had high expectations that he would pick up the project and run with it, and he hasn't. Recently, I assigned two others to help him, but I've waited a while to do it."

For me, this response was a red flag. Bob said in response to step 3 that he was moving fast on the project, yet here he was waiting patiently for Patrick to find his way. When it appeared that Patrick wasn't doing the job, Bob covered for him by assigning two other people to help.

This did not sound like what Bob would have done if he had been on pattern. He is an efficiency genius. He certainly wouldn't assign three people to a job when one ought to be doing it and isn't. I pointed this out to him.

"Well, you're right," Bob said thoughtfully. "Pat's a very smart guy, but he is not the outstanding person who will get personally involved and take the extra step. Furthermore, he has no real logistics experience. He was available for an assignment, and I took him as a favor to my boss Martin. I suppose I could have assigned Patrick to something else, but I gave him this project."

"In my gut, I know Pat's just not the right guy for the job," Bob sighed. "I expected him to push the program, but for whatever reasons—because he didn't have an interest, or didn't understand it, or couldn't do it, or wouldn't—he just hasn't picked up the project and run with it."

I pointed out that this reason for choosing a key employee—either that he was available or as a favor to Bob's boss—was far off pattern for Bob. Indeed, the fact that Bob does not let protocol get in his way in step 3 suggests that he should have refused to take Patrick off his boss's hands.

I pointed out the ruinous effects for Bob that behaving like a good guy had in a situation like this. By taking Patrick as his key employee, Bob wasn't serving either himself or his boss very well.

I asked Bob whether there was someone else in the company who would be better at doing the job of spearheading the base report project. As I expected, Bob answered immediately. "Bruce Mechlenberg, the head of the plant operations group, was the best choice all along," he said. "But he wasn't available, and Pat was there. So I guess that's where I've gone off pattern in all this."

I asked what would have been necessary to get Bruce for the base report project in the first place. Bob acknowledged that it would have been tough. He would have had to pull strings and upset many people. What would have served Bob and his company best in the first place?

Bob agreed that getting Bruce as his key employee for the base report project was what he had wanted to do and what he should have done in the first place. By compromising his pattern, Bob had wasted six months and given his critical project something of a bad name. Now that he knew his pattern, Bob wouldn't make that mistake again.

Bob could see that, once he had the right person in place, the rest of his pattern would flow pretty well. He vowed to find a way to get Bruce assigned to the base report project, whatever he had to do.

We then scanned the remaining items in Bob's pattern just to be sure there were no additional problems that needed attending to. Because these steps had not happened yet, I will not list them in question format.

5. I continually research and plan, research and plan, staying in close touch with all levels of the people involved and the mood of the situation, working to foresee all the problems that could come up, and preparing to meet them.

Bob didn't think that he'd have any trouble with this step. He had been frustrated that not enough had happened yet, and he would get deeply involved once the project was under way and the right person was in place.

6. I insist, even to the point of obstinacy, not just on doing it right but on doing it perfectly.

Again, Bob knew he was all right here. The whole point of his approach was to figure out what *perfect* was and have people work in reference to it. I emphasized that it was important for him not to settle for a half-good job as he had done with Patrick.

7. I personally do whatever is necessary to keep the undertaking going strong, including sitting in the hotseat and taking whatever criticism is directed at me.

Here again, Bob knew that if Bruce was in charge, he'd have no trouble supporting him and taking the heat if something went wrong. With Patrick, he'd been taking a lot of heat for no reason.

8. I make sure that the people involved at all levels know how much I value and care about them by telling them so and by showing a great deal of support in a temperate way.

From Bob's point of view, he had been giving Patrick too much support, to the point where he hadn't been honest about how upset he was with Patrick's performance. If the work was going well, Bob knew that everyone would feel his support.

9. I succeed in pulling the whole thing off and leaving behind a positive, proactive, and self-sustaining operation.

Bob could see that this point was important. He wanted the base report approach to budgeting to be positive, and he wanted the people involved in it to be proactive and able to sustain the vital energy when he had moved on to other things. It would fulfill these conditions if he had the right person. It wouldn't otherwise.

10. I am deeply satisfied with how successful the undertaking has been and by how well everyone has been served.

Bob knew that he would be satisfied once the base report process was in place with Bruce Mechlenberg at its helm.

As in Nick's case, because Bob's pattern described how he did his best work, it was an excellent indicator of what was wrong when a project was not going well. Just my asking whether Bob had taken each step of his pattern with integrity showed Bob exactly what he needed to do to get his project back on track. Then, using the remaining steps of his pattern as a guide, he could determine whether he needed to be alert for other snags.

Bob's example illustrates an important point. Bob had actually gone off pattern in steps 3 and 4. He had compromised for short-term expediency instead of staying true to his pattern—and acting with integrity. Now, six months later, he had to take two steps back and perform steps 3 and 4 correctly. The real world had quickly shown that his compromise approach wasn't going to work.

Avoid Generalizing About Individuals

Please do not draw any generalized conclusions from the preceding example that you should ever compromise in selecting people. There are innumerable people in our data base with patterns very different from Bob's who could have taken Patrick and had the project work well. These people do their best work by developing other people or by responding to the challenge of working with a novice who has great potential. Patrick fit that bill. He just didn't fit Bob's pattern. Bob's whole pattern is about moving very quickly, choosing the best person without letting protocol stand in his way, and getting into the trenches with his people if that is necessary for them to reach their goal. For him and only for him, compromising on Patrick was the wrong thing to do. It threw the entire project off.

Conclusions

In general, compromising your pattern in one of its early steps will come back to haunt you later on. If it is still possible to do so, you will have to return to the earlier step and perform it correctly if you want to get a high-performance outcome. If you no longer have time to go back, you are stuck with grinding out an acceptable result by dint of sheer effort. Bob set off on this path when he assigned two other people to "help" Patrick. In effect, he was trying to produce the result through brute force—in spite of Patrick if necessary. If Bob had been farther down in the hierarchy with fewer resources, he probably would have had to step in and do Patrick's job himself, grinding out some kind of outcome just to avoid embarrassment.

People can compromise about a lot of things. However, patterns identify the factors that are critical for them to produce outstanding results. If they compromise on the critical factors, they end up regretting it. Going back and correcting things after the fact is much more difficult and time-consuming, if it can be done at all, than doing it right in the first place.

8

Deciding Which Job to Go After and Getting It

THE CASE OF THE UNEMPLOYED DIRECTOR OF DEVELOPMENT

In a broad sense, your pattern does not limit you to particular types of jobs or kinds of work. It can give you a way of assessing whether a particular job is a good fit for you and your pattern—whether in that job it will be easy for you to work in the way that is most successful for you. Some goals and some environments make it easier for you to be on pattern than others.

For this example, I selected someone who was out of work and who used her pattern as a guide to deciding between job opportunities. She also used it to plan how to conduct herself in the job interview. It helped her to win the job over a considerable number of competitors.

Although this case is about a person who was out of work, the principles apply perfectly well to someone inside a company who is looking for a different position or to someone whose current assignment has come to an end and who needs a new one.

Beyond identifying the job to apply for, your pattern also helps you to determine what to negotiate for before accepting a job so that once you take it, you can be on pattern and successful. If the prospective employer won't let you work in the way that allows you to be successful, it is better to find that out in advance.

As powerful as the following example is, remember that your pat-

115

tern is really about *how* you do something when you do it very well. It is remarkably independent of *what* you are doing. So if you have decided that you want a particular job, your pattern can tell you how to do it in the way that will work best for you. We have seen many instances of great success when a person has used his or her pattern in a situation that wasn't a natural fit. These people changed the situation so that it better fit their own patterns. By doing so, they created a different way of getting things done. That in turn became a source of great competitive advantage for the organization.

We believe in empowering individuals. We believe that you should decide whether to look for a situation in which you can function easily or choose to work in a situation that must be altered radically if you are to work in accordance with your pattern. No expert should decide that a situation doesn't fit you and your pattern and therefore exclude you from a job because, in the expert's view, you can't be successful. In all too many companies, human resource experts decide what's best for you rather than expect you to take charge of the process. Patterns give you a way of redressing that imbalance of power.

Regina Gold Decides Which Job to Take

Regina Gold had an impressive portfolio of fund-raising successes as director of development for a variety of nonprofit agencies. But she also had an erratic work history. She often had found herself at the center of intense organizational warfare that ultimately threatened her tenure as a fund-raising executive. In the midst of organizational unrest, important board members and agency staff often forgot the dramatic results that Regina's fund-raising plans had produced. When they became too anxious about the details of her partially completed projects, they pulled the plug on Regina's efforts, often at exactly the moment when all the money and energy had been spent but no new funds had yet been raised. At times, Regina had left agency fund-raising positions amid great conflict, without the possibility of finishing the visionary projects that she had originated.

Regina was between jobs when I saw her, having left her previous position in organizational pandemonium with her work under a cloud. She was determined not to get into a position that repeated the same unhappy sequence of events. She needed to understand her own success pattern more completely, and she needed a way of assessing possible jobs and negotiating for what she needed in order to be successful before she had gotten so far into a job that organizational strife threatened her fund-raising efforts.

When Regina Gold looked at the announcements for two new fund-raising jobs for which she qualified, she was uncharacteristically daunted. This was the third time in five years that she had sought a new position, and she wanted to make a good choice. Yet these two jobs were so different from each other that she found it hard to be sure that she was making the right choice or even a good choice for herself.

Regina looked at her High Performance Pattern to help her assess the two job choices and then to help her interview so as to win the job that she wanted.

Regina's Pattern Reveals an Unconventional Visionary

Looking at Regina's pattern, we saw that, at her best, she was an exciting, energetic, visionary person. She could run like crazy with a good idea. However, if she tried to plot all the details before she started a project, she could end up with a boring, grim flop.

Regina's best way of working was, as her pattern describes, quite "bizarre" and unconventional. When we looked at the key aspects of her pattern, we saw that, once Regina got an idea, she made grandiose plans to develop it into a "dream" project that would "right" universal ills.

Then she would set about to put the dream project into place rapidly, acting as if all the necessary resources and support would be there when needed.

When her process was successful, she deliberately became overextended (and feared for her survival), but she also got enough of the dream project into place that others could see its potential and would want to help.

Then she structured the help of the people whom she had attracted so that her castle in the air could settle onto a firm foundation.

High Performance Pattern
for Regina Gold

1. I am asked by someone who knows from experience my capabilities to pull off something that sound exciting and fun. I say yes immediately, making "bizarre" plans and seeing enormous possibilities in what I can do with it.

2. I don't know a lot about the field, but I have had some significant personal experiences, and I see a way in which I can make this an opportunity to right things that I see as universal ills.

3. I digest information gathered from those with direct experience, trust my own experience to sort through the fund of ideas and insights that others have provided, and settle on a small set that hangs together as a dream program.

4. I put all the good ideas into effect as quickly as I can, letting the constraints shift, if necessary, to accommodate what seems right to me.

5. I soon find that I'm overextended, fear for my "survival" and reputation, and devise ingenious and humorous ways to dodge the oncoming bullets.

6. I set up structures that attract people to help, give them plenty of room to contribute and learn from the experience, and watch the castle I've built in the air gradually settle onto a firm foundation.

7. I watch the program grow and regularly add new pieces to fill out the dream.

8. I stop to appreciate and be nurtured by the energy and excitement of the programs I've put into place, taking great pride in showing them off.

9. I receive regular praise and acclaim all along the way, culminating in major official recognition for what I have created.

As you might imagine from a pattern like this, lots of people in a nonprofit organization could become very anxious when Regina was in the initial, very exciting, but totally overextended phase of building a fund-raising operation. If they pulled the plug on resources at this early point in her project, it became very hard for Regina to survive. The overextended operation would collapse without resources and kill the potential that Regina needed in order to attract permanent support.

Once Regina understood her High Performance Pattern, she also understood how anxiety-producing her process could be for someone who managed a small, nonprofit agency. Nevertheless, she wanted to operate according to her pattern because she knew it was exactly how she was most successful. Like the High Performance Patterns that we have already examined, it was written in her own words, and she had personally confirmed that each step in the pattern was authentic.

Regina recognized that, if her employers could trust her in spite of the overextended operations that she created at the start of a project, she would initiate a very imaginative and exciting fund-raising program that would attract supporters who would make fund raising self-sustaining. She also knew that, if she couldn't create an exciting fund-raising enterprise, there was very little that she could do to attract people who would help her raise funds for her employer.

Which Job Should Regina Choose?

As Regina evaluated the two job opportunities, the convenience of one position was tempting. But since the jobs were so different, she wanted to know which situation would be more likely to allow her to perform successfully, that is, in accordance with her pattern.

Within ten minutes' drive of Regina's suburban home, a prominent girls' school sought a chief fund-raising director to carry on a fifty-year tradition of community solicitation. The other job possibility was an hour's drive from Regina's home. There, an innovative national math education program for inner-city youth was seeking a development director to attract corporate and individual contributions so that the program could get started locally.

We started by comparing the two jobs with the key elements of Regina's High Performance Pattern.

Which program could be a dream project to right universal ills? Clearly, an inner-city education program had a better chance of righting universal ills than a suburban girls' school with a fine reputation.

Which program would back up Regina's efforts to develop "bizarre" plans into a grandiose scheme? In a new program with enormous needs and no fund-raising traditions, there could be a real opportunity to develop "bizarre" and unusual fund-raising plans as long as Regina did not need large expenditures to produce results.

At a school with a fifty-year tradition of fund-raising, it was likely that strong fund-raising processes would already be in place, and a newcomer's innovative plans might be resisted, even if they promised to double the institution's funding over time.

Which program would tolerate Regina if she became overextended and used that as a way of attracting people to help her solidify the new fund-raising program? Board members and staff actively working to establish a new inner-city program would probably be more tolerant of an overextended fund-raising executive—and more willing to wait for results.

At an established institution, board members and staff were likely to be more cautious and less amenable to unusual fund-raising methods, particularly if the fund-raising program seemed overextended.

We didn't have to look a lot further. We both could see that, despite the advantages of convenience and stability in the girls' school job near her home, Regina had a much greater chance of staying on pattern with the inner-city education project. There was a much greater chance that she could realize key elements of her pattern with the inner-city project, including righting universal ills, making "bizarre" plans, and waiting until she was somewhat overextended to recruit volunteer assistance.

Regina decided to pursue the inner-city education project.

Using Her Pattern to Get the Job

Once Regina had determined that the inner-city math project was the job that she wanted, she used her pattern to determine how to win the position. She decided that she would do best if she could stay on pattern even during the interview. Regina knew that there would be many candidates, since the program was known nationally, and she wanted to be at her best in the application and interview process to win the job.

How could Regina apply each step of her pattern to doing well at a job interview? Again, a pattern simply provides a number of very important signposts. We looked at Regina's pattern to see what it suggested about how she ought to conduct herself in the interviews. In this case, we looked in detail at every single step, just to make sure that we hadn't missed anything.

> 1. I am asked by someone who knows from experience my capabilities to pull off something that sounds exciting and fun. I say yes immediately, making "bizarre" plans and seeing enormous possibilities in what I can do with it.

Regina decided that, in the interview, she could talk to the interviewers about how exciting and fun this job could be and outline some "bizarre" plans for the fund-raising campaign. She knew that once they told her more about the job and the inner-city math project, her mind would take off, and no other candidate would be able to generate the range of exciting fund-raising campaign ideas that she could produce.

For Regina, this step indicated that she should not play it safe in the job interview. If her mind wasn't stimulated with some "bizarre" or exciting ideas for fund-raising, chances are the job would be wrong for her. If the interviewers didn't respond well to her far-out ideas, it would be better to find out then than to get the job and have everything blow up later on.

> 2. I don't know a lot about the field, but I have had some significant personal experiences, and I see a way in which I can make this an opportunity to right things that I see as universal ills.

Regina realized that she didn't know much about mathematics and that might be a handicap, but it was on pattern for her not to know a lot about the field. The important thing in the job interview was to acknowledge her relevant experience, which were a Ph.D. in education from Harvard and her experience running and raising money for a ballet school that she had started several years before.

More important, this item suggested that, to be on pattern in the interview, Regina needed to talk about her values, about the ills that this program could cure and why she believed that working for the program was the right thing to do. She did believe that mathematics was critical, that the lack of mathematical skill was a significant barrier for minorities and women seeking jobs and promotions. She also believed that the program had potential for helping minorities and women (including herself) to overcome some of these barriers.

> 3. I digest information gathered from those with direct experience, trust my own experience to sort through the fund of ideas and insights that others have provided, and settle on a small set that hangs together as a dream program.

Applying this step of her pattern to the interview process, Regina decided that she would carefully listen to the interviewers' ideas and experiences, questioning them about their concepts of the program. Then she would reformulate her initial "bizarre" fund-raising ideas on the spot, synthesizing the interviewers' ideas with her own. She had no doubts that she could do this.

Creating such syntheses out of brainstorming sessions was one of Regina's strengths. Without the guidance of her pattern, however, she doubted that it would have been as clear to her that she ought to use (and demonstrate) the skill at the interview.

> 4. I put all the good ideas into effect as quickly as I can, letting the constraints shift, if necessary, to accommodate what seems right to me.

Applying this step of her pattern, Regina realized that this was going to be the gutsiest place in the interview process. This step suggested that, to be at her best, Regina needed to present her synthesis in an organized way to the interviewers, saying, "Here is what would be good to do, and it is what I would do if I had the job."

Regina realized that she had to risk letting the interviewers know just what she would really do in the job and trust that they wouldn't be scared away. At the same time, she had to trust that, if the interviewers were frightened by her responses, the job wasn't the one that she should take.

> 5. I soon find that I'm overextended, fear for my "survival" and reputation, and devise ingenious and humorous ways to dodge the oncoming bullets.

This step suggested that Regina should expect some negative reaction from the interviewers at first. In fact, if she didn't get any, she probably hadn't been as original and far-out as she needed to be. If and when the interviewers started shooting Regina's ideas down, she should be sure to respond with humor and imagination until they began to come round to her side.

> 6. I set up structures that attract people to help, give them plenty of room to contribute and learn from the experience, and watch the castle I've built in the air gradually settle onto a firm foundation.

Once the interviewers had expressed some interest in Regina's approach, this pattern step suggested that she should move to enlist them, pointing out how they could participate in such a successful fund-raising effort. By this time, they should want to hire her so that they could participate in her dream.

Regina was at this point quite visibly excited by the prospect of going into the interview. She felt that she had a way of conducting herself in the interview that would win the interviewers over to her.

> 7. I watch the program grow and regularly add new pieces to fill out the dream.

If the interview has gone well to this point, this step in Regina's pattern suggested to us that the interviewers would be contributing ideas about how Regina's model of a fund-raising program could work. Each time an interviewer proposed another fund-raising idea, Regina should add it to her conception.

> 8. I stop to appreciate and be nurtured by the energy and excitement of the programs I've put into place, taking great pride in showing them off.

This step indicated that, toward the end of the interview, Regina should talk to the interviewers about what they had created with her during the interview and express great hopes that she would be hired to help move these ideas to completion. She should also encourage the interviewers by reminding them of what they would be able to do if they chose to hire her and let her run with their fund-raising plan.

9. I receive regular praise and acclaim all along the way, culminating in major official recognition for what I've created.

Regina realized that, if she could keep the interview going and follow the guidelines laid out by her pattern, the interviewers would be excited, and she would be offered the job. The official recognition, of course, would be the job offer.

Regina Wins the Job

Within two weeks of meeting with Regina, we received a very large floral bouquet with a note thanking us for her High Performance Pattern and for our help in applying it. Regina's job interview had gone almost exactly as we had planned. By the end, the interviewers enthusiastically recommended that the inner-city math project hire her immediately so that they could get on with her fund-raising programs.

Regina was hired as development director of the education program for inner-city youth the following day.

General Principles

Most people can see just by reading Regina's pattern how it could be applied to her work in developing significant fund-raising projects. Applying it to her process of choosing a job or to the aim of succeeding at a job interview further illustrates the power of High Performance Patterns and the way in which they are not limited to particular types of situations.

A pattern can show an individual how to act in any situation. But each new situation presents an intellectual challenge. Just as we had to ascertain what each step in Regina's pattern meant in the context of a job interview, you must figure out what each step means in the new situation. Then resolve to act that way when you're in that situation.

Please do not generalize from one person to another. Regina has a very unique, high-risk way of behaving when she is on pattern, and that is what works for her. Thus, she had to control the interview process enough to put herself on the spot and come through under pressure. She did, and she was great at it, and she won the job. People who have different patterns should conduct themselves quite differently in job interviews if they want to win. However, the underlying principle remains the same: Find a way to be on pattern in the situation, and you have the maximum possibility of being successful.

9

Finding Time for the Family While Holding a Demanding Executive Position

THE CASE OF THE JOB-COMES-FIRST EXECUTIVE

One of the more difficult tasks that a busy executive faces is to carve out time for family and personal life. With competitive pressures, there is always more to do or more that can be done.

Most executives know that they need some balance in their lives. They cannot work sixty-hour weeks and really be maximally effective. It just seems that, at any given moment, business demands take the higher priority. Regardless of the resolve to spend more time with family and children, that priority is neglected. It is also fairly evident that, for many reasons, neglecting one's personal and family life is not wise. As one friend noted, "No one ever says on his deathbed, 'I wish I had worked harder.' But lots of people say, 'I wish I had spent more time with my spouse and children.'" All too often, it takes a heart attack or other serious illness to straighten out one's priorities—assuming that one even gets a second chance.

This case in this chapter shows how one executive used his High Performance Pattern to create a plan for a family vacation that was so high on his list of priorities that, when last-minute business pressures threatened to derail it, he went on vacation anyway. The solution involves what we have come to call *projectizing* a fuzzy goal. It is a way of turning a vague yearning into something that you can do something about.

Jack Grand Figures Out How to Have a Family Vacation

As vice president of a regional power company, Jack Grand had primary responsibility for presenting rate adjustment requests to the state public utilities commission. In addition to preparing exacting financial data in a precise format, Jack was required to meet commission deadlines for submitting materials and to make presentations on behalf of the company at formal, quasi-legal hearings. He also carefully maintained business and social relationships with his company's executive staff as well as with staff members of the commission.

Jack's work was structured in a way that fit him very well. He enjoyed what he did, and when he was most successful, it meant millions of dollars of profit for the company. He was definitely a fast-rising executive in the company. But Jack felt that he spent far too much time away from his family.

"I can get real caught up in my work and almost forget to come home at times," Jack explained, "and, too often, that keeps me from spending time with my wife, our five-year-old boy, and our baby daughter."

Jack was a dedicated family man—he really did want to spend much more time with his wife and his two young children. He just couldn't seem to make it work. We started, of course, by looking at Jack's pattern.

Jack's Project: "Spending Time with My Family"

Jack's pattern revealed that the key was to make a project out of something. Then he would approach it with the same discipline with which he approached any business goal. So I suggested *Spend More Time with My Wife and Children* as one of Jack's priority projects. He laughed— and then recognized that he might be able to use the approach successfully if he did just that. It was a question of structuring time with his family so that, when the normal business emergencies threatened to intervene, he would still see time with his family as having the higher priority.

We could both see from the first step in his pattern that Jack was at his best when he worked on short-term, dramatic projects that had

High Performance Pattern
for Jack Grand

1. I am part of a project team preparing for a periodic but dramatic high-stakes event with a definite outcome; we will either succeed or fail.

2. I overcome my initial uncertainties by learning the existing process of preparation from others more experienced than me, working with it until I can carry it out more thoroughly than ever; then I feel I understand why it's done that way.

3. I sense that something is not right about our current approach, identify the issue in question, and convince the rest of the team that the potential benefit is great enough to free up some time for me to find a better solution.

4. I consult experts, read, and otherwise assimilate information relevant to the issue and let it all simmer until I have a key insight: I know what's wrong and what to do about it.

5. I work step by step through the data available, preparing a complete package to convince the others on the team that this is the right way to approach the issue.

6. I get the team's excited support of my new approach, and we rearrange every piece of work that we've done like a giant jigsaw puzzle into a practical system that relies on my insight.

7. I enter the event itself with great empathy and understanding for the positions of others, actively suggesting my solutions, accommodating their concerns as well as my own, and trading off on legitimate differences of opinion.

8. I watch the event go the way I want, and I am elated by how well we do.

9. I realize that my performance is noted by those who have a say over my future, and I am presented with an even greater opportunity as a result.

high-stakes results. According to Jack's pattern, then, the key was to make time with his family into a series of dramatic, short-term projects involving his wife and children that had high-stakes results. Could he do that?

Jack's first thought was that it would be impossible for him to make time with his family into a dramatic high-stakes project. He found it difficult to imagine that he could maintain commitments to his family if business emergencies intervened. But I encouraged him to find out what his pattern revealed when it was applied to his family. As I put it, "Let's work through your pattern and figure out what it suggests. You can always then decide not to do it." He agreed. Together, we analyzed Jack's "time with my family" project step by step, using his pattern as the guide.

1. I am part of a project team preparing for a dramatic high-stakes event with a definite outcome; we will either succeed or fail.

This was the key element of the pattern for Jack's "time with my family" project. I asked Jack to consider what dramatic activities he might do with his wife and children that would be high-stakes in the sense that family interaction would be high and family members would have a chance to get to know one another better. I also suggested that a good plan would require the family activity to be marked on his calendar each month to focus the time that they spent together and to ensure that they kept it up.

"All kinds of things come to mind," Jack exclaimed. "I've always wanted to buy a boat, and we could plan for a three- or four-day sail every month. We could go on a trip! We could take a skiing vacation. I guess what you're suggesting is that my family becomes like the project team," he concluded.

I pointed out that, to be on pattern, Jack needed a specific project and a specific date in order to make it an event that they could prepare for. He agreed and selected a family vacation in Hawaii—something he and his wife had been talking about for years—as the first high-stakes family time project.

2. I overcome my initial uncertainties by learning the existing process of preparation from others more experienced than me,

working with it until I can carry it out more thoroughly than ever; then I feel I understand why it's done that way.

Because when Jack is on pattern he prepares thoroughly and learns from experts, I asked how he could follow this step with respect to the Hawaiian vacation

"I guess my family and I would consult other people when we were planning our dramatic activity," Jack responded. "That could be a travel agent or someone who's bought a condo there and spends a lot of time on the islands. I know several people who would be good on both scores. All this suggests is that I listen to these people and plan my own vacation with my family even more thoroughly." I concurred.

3. I sense that something is not right about our current approach, identify the issue in question, and convince the rest of the team that the potential benefit is great enough to free up some time for me to find a better solution.

Jack's instinct told him that he needed to do more than just plan the trip. I proposed that he trust his nose for weak spots when he was making plans for the trip and that he take the time to resolve any questions that arose every time he felt this way.

I asked him what he thought some of the issues in question might be, as best as he could identify them now. First, he said, what satisfied his two young children didn't always satisfy him or his wife. I agreed that that might be so, but I said that a good travel agent could suggest ways of handling that problem.

Then Jack revealed what was really bothering him. "I've planned trips before and cancelled them at the last minute when things became hot and heavy at work. There has to be more at stake." I pointed out that he was right on pattern. We had started the planning and something was not right. Here he identified it.

We both agreed that this was critical. I reminded him of step 1 in his pattern. Making the vacation high-stakes was crucial—Jack had to have more to lose by cancelling the vacation than by dealing with any work crisis that might arise. The key was how to increase the stakes.

I suggested that Jack keep this in mind when he was planning, but since this step in his pattern allowed him to buy time, he did not need to decide immediately how to increase what was at stake on this trip.

4. I consult experts, read, and otherwise assimilate information relevant to the issue and let it all simmer until I have the key insight: I know what's wrong and what to do about it.

If some part of Jack's preparation didn't seem quite right, this step suggested that the family should consult experts to get beyond difficulties. It also suggested that, in the face of some problem, he shouldn't jump at the first solution. At his best, he took time to mull things over. This approach ultimately led to a key insight about how to solve it.

I asked Jack what expert he could consult about increasing the stakes on his vacation so he couldn't back out. A travel agent might not be a good resource on this question. Jack recalled that another executive in his company always managed to take his vacations. Jack figured he could consult with him.

5. I work step by step through the data available, preparing a complete package to convince the others on the team that this is the right way to approach the issue.

6. I get the team's excited support of my new approach, and we rearrange every piece of the work that we've done like a giant jigsaw puzzle into a practical system that relies on my insight.

These two steps seemed to go together in planning the family vacation. Once Jack found a twist that could make the stakes high enough that he couldn't cancel the vacation, he would have to convince his family that they ought to adopt the twist as part of their vacation plan. Then he could integrate the twist into the plan.

I suggested that the plan for Jack's family vacation should include the responsibilities that each family member, including the children, would have, just as a business plan would. This move would make family members part of the project team.

7. I enter the event itself with great empathy and understanding for the positions of the others, actively suggesting my solutions, accommodating their concerns as well as my own, and trading off on legitimate differences of opinion.

We decided that this step in Jack's pattern applied to how he should interact with the members of his family during the vacation. When Jack has done his preparation thoroughly, his plans do accommodate the legitimate concerns of others.

Jack found this very helpful. "So I just need to be my normal self in this instance," said Jack. "I should listen to the needs and positions of other members of my family and try to take them into account." He knew he had a tendency not to listen to what his children wanted, and this step in his pattern suggested he needed to make trade-offs with them as well as with his wife. I suggested that he make a particular point of listening to his children's wishes.

8. I watch the event go the way I want, and I am elated by how well we do.

In this case, the elation would be the result of close contact between Jack and his children or between Jack and his wife. Since that's what he wanted as the result of spending time together, the trip should fit his pattern perfectly.

9. I realize that my performance is noted by those who have a say over my future, and I am presented with an even greater opportunity as a result.

This step foresees the reaction of the other members of Jack's family when he pulls the vacation off really well. The real proof here would be that, if all went well, the rest of Jack's family would begin to suggest additional things to do for time with family projects.

How the Vacation Plan Worked for Jack and His Family

Shortly after I worked with Jack, he and his family created the vacation project, using Jack's pattern as their framework. They spent a full week in Hawaii, rented a sailboat, and enjoyed a full schedule of boating and tourist events.

In the course of their planning, Jack and his family realized that the high-stakes element in Jack's pattern meant being fully committed in some way so that not following through would have significant consequences. They decided that, to combat Jack's tendency to put work first, they would fully commit to their Hawaiian holiday in advance. They bought nonrefundable airline tickets and put down deposits on the rental of a condominium, sailboat, and car. Then to make their plans even more difficult to change, they extended an invitation to their five-year-old son's best friend. If a crisis arose, cancellation would be much more difficult when another five-year-old and his family were involved.

Two days before the departure date, Jack's office faced an unexpected crisis. Ordinarily, he would have rolled up his sleeves and joined the fray. But the "spending time with my family" project had a higher-stakes priority. Jack left for his vacation despite the crisis, and, as he later learned, his staff managed perfectly well without him.

In Jack's case, not only did his pattern guide him to the first real vacation that he had had with his family in years, but he also developed a good plan for creating family time that could work on an ongoing basis.

When he returned from Hawaii, Jack put together a presentation to convince his boss that he should take regular three- and four-day weekends with his family as compensatory time for the inhuman hours that he put in when preparing rate case presentations. His boss agreed to Jack's proposal, and when Jack and I last talked he and his family were busily planning one long weekend a month and committing fully to each one so that no one could back out.

Making a Critical Goal a Project

High Performance Patterns work well when applied to personal situations. Figuring out what each step of the pattern means in a nonbusiness context can pose a problem and require some creative interpretation, but it is almost always possible. Deciding what to do in the situation to be on pattern involves extensive brainstorming and creative thinking, but when the key idea emerges, the person always knows it is right.

As a rule, people who cannot seem to make headway on something that they vaguely want to do need to make the desire more concrete to prompt them to action. A good first step is the one that Jack used: make a project out of the desire. Then, whether your objective is personal or professional, you can usually determine quite easily how your pattern applies. Patterns are very concrete and practical.

Jack's case illustrates another benefit of applying patterns. At first, Jack couldn't imagine how he could create a high-stakes family project that would take priority over his business demands, although that was what he wanted. When he had the initial doubts, I merely suggested that we work through the pattern together and see what we could come up with in response to its guidance. He could always decide later not to do it. As with most creative activities, taking a somewhat hypothetical attitude toward the activity helps people shed their limited thinking. The freedom not to act frees them to come up with unique solutions. Usually the results are so convincing that they eagerly plunge ahead.

10

Making the Best of the Only Job Available in a Downsizing

THE CASE OF THE ENGINEER FORCED TO TURN SALESMAN

Sometimes your employment situation is less than ideal. All the cards seem stacked against success, but for personal reasons you decide to stay on. Then your challenge is to make the best of a job that doesn't fit. How can someone make the best of a situation that seems not to fit his or her High Performance Pattern? What could knowledge of the pattern add? How can the person find a way of achieving high performance despite the constraints of an inhospitable situation?

The Field Services Manager Turns Salesman

For ten years, Mike Draker was the well-respected field services manager of Shamrock Power, a manufacturer of large diesel power generators. Located in Denver, he directed a maintenance staff of eight, who provided field service for company-built generators on the West Coast. Trained as an engineer, Mike was comfortable in his job. It fit his pattern well, and customers liked his work.

When the Shamrock Power company reorganized and eliminated the area service center that he managed, Mike faced a difficult choice. A sales position was the only job opening in Denver, and Mike had no previous experience in sales. Should he relocate to Seattle for a new field services management position? Or should he take a district sales position with Shamrock in order to remain in Denver, where his wife was employed and his children were in school?

After considering job prospects with Shamrock in other parts of the United States, gathering information, and discussing the choices with his family and his boss, Mike decided that he wanted to continue working for Shamrock. But he also realized that keeping his family in the Denver area was his top priority. He decided to start a new career as a Shamrock Power district salesman based in Denver.

Mike wondered how he could approach this new, unfamiliar job as a salesman in a way that would be consistent with his pattern. Although sales was a totally unfamiliar arena for him, we were able to use Mike's pattern to analyze a specific sales situation with Acme Tires. Not only did we come up with high-performance solutions to Acme's needs, we also identified the approach to selling that fit Mike and would give him a striking competitive advantage.

Applying Mike's Pattern to Making a Big-Ticket Sale at Acme Tires

Mike began by looking at a prospective sale to Acme Tires, a dissatisfied customer saddled with Shamrock equipment that often broke down. Three years before, Acme had purchased a generator from a Shamrock salesman. One of the expensive heating elements in this generator repeatedly burned out during normal plant operations. Mike and his field service team had visited Acme Tires on many occasions to replace the heating element and repair the generator. Acme argued that the generator had been improperly designed. They wanted Shamrock to give them a free replacement system. Mike felt that a free replacement was out of the question—although Acme had reason to be upset, it had approved the generator's specs in the first place.

How could Mike solve Acme's equipment problem and use that as an opportunity to sell them additional equipment? Would Mike's pattern indicate the best ways to approach the sale?

Point-by-Point Brainstorming

As with the preceding cases, we began by examining Mike's pattern, step by step. This process was somewhat more complicated in Mike's

High Performance Pattern for Mike Draker

1. I realize a situation is not working and try to improve it for all involved, although at first I don't clearly see how.
2. I gather information about what to do from all resources that I can identify, building my knowledge base by listening to and internalizing the experience of others and without taking any one thing as gospel.
3. I find a person who supports me that I can bounce my thoughts and ideas off of; this lets me air my thoughts and internally work through the possibilities until they crystallize into a vision that is obviously the right thing to do—the path that I should follow.
4. I realize it would be stupid to go any other way. I take the initiative to set off on the new path, coordinating the pieces and taking the first action steps necessary to begin the new project.
5. I involve myself with all aspects of the project, continually being aware of individual and technical needs and meeting them while making sure that the whole will come together the way it should in order to work best.
6. I treat people the way I would want to be treated if I were in their shoes. I honor their struggle to do their job the way they feel they have to do it until they become fully responsible for doing it right.
7. I help overcome any obstacles that surface by digging into the problem further with the people involved, helping them talk about it and understand it until an obvious resolution surfaces that is fair to all sides.
8. I find that each phase leads to new ideas that I build into the next phases. Each step expands the vision further until the whole project goes far beyond what I had foreseen.
9. I achieve visible proof that I have successfully created a deeper level of high quality, and the measurement continues to be true through time.
10. I receive subtle and validating expressions of my value and contribution from those who benefit by the deeper level of quality that we have achieved.
11. I find I have experienced and become clear about another part of myself and in the process gained a valuable insight that I will remember and continue to use in the future.

case, however, because we had a twofold objective. That is, we examined each step for what it indicated on the one hand as Mike's best approach to selling in general, and on the other about Mike's handling of the Acme Tires situation.

> 1. I realize a situation is not working and try to improve it for all
> involved, although at first I don't clearly see how.

The first step told us that Mike works best in a situation involving an ongoing problem that needs a better resolution for all participants, a resolution that has yet to be recognized.

It was simple to apply this step to selling: Mike would be best at selling when the customer had an ongoing problem and Mike could help the customer arrive at an outstanding and equitable solution. By definition, this solution would include purchasing new equipment or services.

By this understanding, Acme Tires was an ideal sales situation for Mike. There was a serious ongoing problem, and Mike was involved (now as a salesman, before as field services manager). Mike also wanted the situation to be better for all concerned, so that Acme and Shamrock could continue to do business and trust each other in the future.

The first step in Mike's pattern also suggested a general approach to selling. If there was no obvious ongoing customer problem, Mike should ask what problem the customer would like new equipment to solve. Once a problem had been identified, Mike could help the customer arrive at an even better solution than any that he might have been considering.

> 2. I gather information about what to do from all resources that I
> can identify, building my knowledge base by listening to and
> internalizing the experience of others and without taking any
> one thing as gospel.

This step suggested that, when Mike was on pattern and therefore most effective, he built his knowledge base about a problem in a very open-minded and thorough way. He literally attempted to internalize the experience of the other people involved.

At Acme, then, Mike should begin by building his knowledge

base. He already knew something of the history, but as field services manager he had not been able to intervene to provide a better solution. Now, with responsibility for selling, he could. As we explored how he could approach Acme in a way that was consistent with this step of his pattern, Mike began to describe the information he needed.

He wanted to know, he said, what range of solutions Acme was willing to look at, what the current costs for replacement parts and downtime were, and how much Acme was prepared to spend on a solution. He also decided to ask Acme what approach they would take if Shamrock were not involved. His pattern suggested that Mike should also gather information from other sources. When I asked him to name some, he indicated that he could ask a Shamrock engineer to visit Acme for a first-hand look at the problem. He could also ask Shamrock design engineers about the design of the initial product and alternative engineering solutions.

Most important, Mike's pattern made it clear that he should not adopt anyone's solution at this point in the process. To be on pattern with Acme, he just needed to listen and internalize. And that is an extremely effective selling technique that Mike could use with other sales prospects: really listen to the customer instead of pushing a line of products.

> 3. I find a person who supports me that I can bounce my thoughts and ideas off of; this lets me air my thoughts and internally work through the possibilities until they crystallize into a vision that is obviously the right thing to do—the path that I should follow.

We both realized that this step was a critical element for Mike. Once he had internalized all the information about his customer's situation, he needed to bounce his thoughts and ideas off of someone he knew he could trust. His pattern suggested that, by doing this, he would crystallize a realistic solution that was right for the situation. I asked Mike who might serve as this key support person.

This was the first problem that we faced when applying Mike's pattern to the selling environment. As field services manager, his district manager had filled the sounding board role. After a service call, the two of them would kick around the information Mike had gathered, and eventually the right approach would emerge. But when the field services center was closed, the district manager had relocated. As a salesman, Mike needed to develop a new support network to help him crystallize alternatives into a vision of the right thing to do.

As we talked, Mike's sales supervisor emerged as a possibility. He considered the Shamrock salesman who had preceded him on the Acme account, but he feared that that man's support could soon turn into antagonism if Mike insisted on a complete replacement of the equipment at Acme. In any case, Mike knew that finding a strong support person in his new situation had a high priority.

> 4. I realize it would be stupid to go any other way. I take the initiative to set off on the new path, coordinating the pieces and taking the first action steps necessary to begin the new project.

This step would be where Mike actually presented a sales proposal to the customer. With respect to Acme, he would need a proposal that said, "Here are the alternatives, and here is the obvious thing you need to do." His proposal would outline the recommended solution, indicate the proportion of costs that Shamrock would pick up and the proportion that would be borne by Acme.

Mike's pattern suggests that, as soon as he has the right idea, he should present it, even if it doesn't quite fit what the customer thinks he or she wants. When Mike is on pattern, he gives people the solution that obviously is right, whether they have considered it or not.

> 5. I involve myself with all aspects of the project, continually being aware of individual and technical needs and meeting them while making sure that the whole will come together the way it should in order to work best.

The more we talked about this step, the more we both felt that it could become a major sales strength for Mike. It would be an advantage to his customers that Mike is an engineer with maintenance experience. Other salespeople could say they would be responsible for equipment installation, but few if any had Mike's direct experience in maintenance. Mike should emphasize that point when trying to make a sale.

This step suggested to us that, if Acme ordered new equipment,

Mike should stay on top of the project during installation. In that way, he could promise Acme (and other customers) that equipment would be installed in the best possible way and that he would be ready to deal with any problems that arose.

> 6. I treat people the way I would want to be treated if I were in their shoes. I honor their struggle to do their job the way they feel they have to do it until they become fully responsible for doing it right.

This step, we felt, was another sales strength for Mike: He naturally looked at the situation from the customer's point of view and took their concerns seriously until they were satisfied with the final result. In a sales situation, the customer could expect that Mike would work hard to understand his or her business and to make sure that the products served its ends.

> 7. I help overcome any obstacles that surface by digging into the problem further with the people involved, helping them talk about it and understand it until an obvious resolution surfaces that is fair to all sides.

This step was critical to the way Mike worked best. Now he needed to incorporate it into how he would sell. Mike should keep talking with everyone concerned—even after the initial sale was made—to ensure that all needs were met and that any problems that arose during installation would be resolved to the satisfaction of all sides. Needless to say, for Mike to be an effective salesperson, Shamrock would have to support his effort to follow projects through to completion.

> 8. I find that each phase leads to new ideas that I build into the next phases. Each step expands the vision further until the whole project goes far beyond what I had foreseen.

This is the way Mike works best in any situation. In selling, it would become the basis for add-on sales. This step, combined with others, revealed that Mike's ideal selling process was one of getting something going initially with a client and then watching as the situation unfolded. Each piece would suggest new ideas for the next phase, which Mike would then put together and present to the client. Mike's ideal client would have an ongoing problem that required a big-ticket Shamrock Power item with strong potential for add-on sales as part of its solution. This would make it worth the time that Mike took to solve his client's problems.

At Acme, Mike needed to help resolve the problem with the existing equipment as the first step. Then, as Acme and Shamrock began putting that resolution into place (a resolution that incorporated new Shamrock equipment), Mike could identify other upgrading needs for Acme's operations. Each upgrade would be an additional sale for Mike. Needless to say, Mike was delighted with the evolving sales strategy.

9. I achieve visible proof that I have successfully created a deeper level of high quality, and the measurement continues to be true through time.

At his best, Mike devises a high-quality, lasting solution. With respect to selling, his satisfied customer would sign off on the project and continue to be satisfied with Mike's solution for a long time afterward. It took some effort on my part to convince Mike that this was a powerful selling strategy. What better recommendation could he have than customers who were satisfied because, when Mike sold them something, their problem not only was solved, but it stayed solved? However, this placed an extra burden on him in the situation at Acme. He would have to work out a solution between Shamrock and Acme that was not just a temporary fix. I emphasized—and Mike understood—how crucial it was to his success that he be true to this aspect of how he worked best.

10. I receive subtle and validating expressions of my value and contribution from those who benefit by the deeper level of quality that we have achieved.

In Mike's high-performance experiences, he received many subtle validating expressions from the beneficiaries. Now he needed to learn how to recognize these validations in selling situations. As we talked, Mike realized that, at his best, he wouldn't just be selling a product. He would be creating rapport and trust and selling the idea that the customer should do business with him on an ongoing basis. This approach directly contradicted what the introductory sales courses had taught him. But it fit him much better.

11. I find I have experienced and become clear about another part of myself and in the process gained a valuable insight that I will remember and continue to use in the future.

It is important for Mike to "learn" something from each experience that he can remember and continue to use. That is how his high-performance experiences end when they end right. In selling, this meant that he needed to make sure that he continued to pull insights from each sale experience. Mike said he felt this would not be hard to do. He would learn plenty over the next few years.

Mike's Pattern Provides New Insights

After considering the relation between his pattern and the concrete selling situation at Acme Tires, Mike felt much better about his ability to do well as a salesman. His High Performance Pattern had made him very effective as a field service manager, and now he could see how it could be applied directly to sales. Many aspects of Mike's pattern would cause customers to identify with him and believe that he would treat them very well.

It was not difficult to figure out how to make Mike's pattern work well in a selling situation. The key was to get Shamrock to allow Mike to take major responsibility for overseeing the work of implementation after products were sold. Customers in big-ticket selling often expect the salesperson to play that role, whether he or she is good at it or not. There is no doubt that Mike would be very good at it indeed—he could use that assurance as a strong competitive advantage when convincing customers to buy from him.

Shortly after we worked through this example, Mike worked out a solution to Acme's problem, the cost of which was split equitably between Shamrock and Acme. When the equipment changes were under way, a number of opportunities arose for upgrading Acme's existing equipment. Mike did very well selling Acme the add-ons. More important, Mike turned a valued but disgruntled customer into a satisfied advocate. He has now been in the job for more than three years, quite successfully.

General Principles

It has been our experience that even when a person's High Performance Pattern does not seem at first to fit a particular scenario, one or two key insights can reveal how to make an inhospitable situation work well for the individual concerned. Working through a specific example while using the High Performance Pattern as a guide can illuminate these insights when they might otherwise remain hidden.

In Mike's case, the key elements were making his installation experience a part of the sales effort at Acme and working to resolve the ongoing problem at Acme so that additional sales could result from upgrades during the solution phase. These sales concepts are not new, but they are the ones that will work for Mike in this sales situation. From these specific ideas, we could extrapolate ways in which Mike could work well in other sales situations.

It is always the particular actions that best fit a particular situation that are so difficult to discern. High Performance Patterns work well to identify this fit, both for the person responsible and for the situation.

11

Finding an Unconventional Niche That Fits

THE CASE OF THE FAILING INSURANCE SALESMAN

People in an organization often find themselves subjected to the organization's belief that there is only one way to be successful. Conceptions of one right way to do things are organizational sacred cows. The logic of this conventional wisdom often seems unassailable at first hearing. It takes considerable courage to do something different from what the organization's most successful people emphasize. This is especially true when you are new on the job. In the imitative phase of learning, you have very little choice but to follow the company line. But what if the company procedure doesn't work for you? Your organization regards you as the failure. It doesn't question its own rigid system of operating. You tend to concur—this foolproof methodology doesn't work for you. Obviously, there is something wrong with you. Right? Wrong! Unfortunately, keeping your confidence under threat of dismissal feels impossible. None of us does his or her best work when we feel like failures *and* we are required to function in a way that is significantly off pattern for us.

Ironically, people often achieve significant breakthroughs precisely by sidestepping standard company procedures. Conversely, significant failures or lost opportunities nearly always result when companies hold on to ideas that are too narrow or whose time has passed. Industry examples of this syndrome are legion. For instance, American manufacturers always cherished the belief that higher quality had to cost more. Then the Japanese demonstrated that higher quality was always cheaper in the end. In so doing, they captured much of the car market. Who do you think lost the market that the Japanese won? In the early years of automotive manufacturing, Henry Ford produced only black cars. Then General Motors began producing cars in various colors. It captured market share and set a trend for the future. Wang stuck to its proprietary operating system far too long—and missed the personal computer revolution. This list of conventional wisdom's disastrous blunders could go on and on.

High Performance Patterns suggest lines of action that fit a person well. Often, these actions contradict conventional wisdom. It is striking how often an unconventional approach works outstandingly well, much to the consternation of people who said that it wouldn't. If managers and executives properly understand this power of High Performance Patterns, they will welcome the ability to identify overlooked niches and unusually powerful ways of making use of people. After all, it is very difficult in any situation to step outside the box that you are in and see its limitations with fresh eyes. Patterns provide fresh perspectives and insights. If a performance-improvement tool merely suggests what you already know or something that is consistent with conventional wisdom, it contributes little. Patterns have the power to break through conventional thinking.

I will illustrate this fact with a case in which a person's pattern suggested that he would be successful doing something that everyone else had rejected as senseless. This case also underscores the importance of being true to oneself when using patterns. If managers and executives begin to understand that honoring the integrity of another person's success pattern will help them uncover much more powerful ways of using people and in many cases alert them to opportunities that their conventional lenses have missed, they will appreciate the great potential of diversity. High Performance Patterns are a practical tool that you can employ to make sure that all the wisdom of your people is being used.

The Man Who Went Against Conventional Wisdom

Joe Porter might accurately be described as streetwise. A somewhat rough personality, he had dropped out of high school, joined the Navy, and for several years during the 1960s travelled the country in a hippie van. He got his high school equivalency degree in the Navy and, after he settled down, started in the insurance business by selling supplementary health insurance door to door. With his unpolished style and genuine concern for people, he sold well to the people who are often home during the day, and he racked up a significant record. Over the years, Joe had worked his way up through five different companies and was finally an agent for one of the top U.S. insurance companies, State Mutual. One thing was clear from his record: Joe could sell.

But at State Mutual, Joe found that, for the first time in his life, his sales results were abysmal. Approximately six months into the year, he ranked forty-seventh out of forty-eight agents working from that office. When at a meeting of agents I was introduced as providing a service that they could use, Joe jumped at the chance. Working for State Mutual had been a dream that he had pursued for years. Now he needed to know what was going wrong, or the company would drop him.

Joe and I set about to find his High Performance Pattern—to understand what he had been doing in comparison to it and to get a sense of his current work environment. As we talked, he told me what the company and the other top agents in the office had been recommending he do. Their advice amounted to the conventional wisdom espoused in the office.

Succinctly stated, everyone agreed that, in the competitive insurance business, there was no money to be made by selling standard products, many of which had low margins and commissions. To make big bucks, you had to contact doctors, lawyers, and other wealthy people, selling insurance as part of an investment/tax deferment package. In effect, to be a top agent, you needed to become a financial adviser to wealthy people.

Joe had attempted to imitate this approach to success. He had worked hard to make contact with successful businesspeople and with wealthy professionals, as State Mutual suggested. He had prepared direct mail letters, made follow-up calls, and scheduled personal visits, all to no avail. For all practical purposes, he had sold nothing for six months.

High Performance Pattern
for Joe Porter

1. I become involved in doing something that helps people who really need help—people who have been disadvantaged by the system.

2. I commit myself to meeting a tangible goal for helping them that has a specific deadline, with immediate and significant personal consequences if I fail.

3. I develop a partner relationship with the person or persons who need help, so that they feel they want to work with me toward the same goal.

4. I and my partners recognize that they are novices who have never before tried to do what we've agreed to do and that I have enough insights and expertise in the subject to be listened to.

5. I make an up-front agreement with my partners about what each of us will contribute to the effort and what each of us expects to get at the end.

6. I bring my special expertise to bear on the situation, and my partners show that they trust me and respect my expertise by doing what I suggest.

7. I arrange for all the support I need for my work with my partners and feel it kick in as things swing into gear.

8. I stay alert to real opportunities that open up, and as I suggest some risks that can take advantage of them, I get my partners' total agreement, so that we share the responsibility if something goes wrong.

9. I follow through thoroughly on everything that I begin and watch the genuine amazement and then gratefulness on the part of the people whom I'm helping as they are treated justly for the first time.

How could Joe use his High Performance Pattern to improve his sales results? Could he sell insurance in a way that fit him and still survive in this top-rated company?

By following the signposts of Joe's own success pattern, we were able to figure out what was wrong—where Joe had gone off track and what he needed to change to get back onto his pattern of success. As a result, Joe improved his sales performance dramatically. In this case, as in others, I had to interpret the pattern broadly. Together, we had to discern how it applied to the context in which Joe was working.

Now let us look at each item in turn to see how Joe can get back on pattern and become successful at selling.

> 1. I become involved in doing something that helps people who really need help—people who have been disadvantaged by the system.

This is a key element of Joe's pattern, because it is what hooks him in. He is instinctively attracted to helping people who have the cards stacked against them. Given his own upbringing and his days as a hippie, this is not surprising. Several of his high-performance stories involved stepping in to help someone who was about to go under. Joe knew how to connect with the disenfranchised. What did this mean in the context of selling insurance? We decided that it meant he needed to be selling some kind of insurance that would protect people who ordinarily have no protection. Doctors, lawyers, other professionals, and highly successful people—the clients that State Mutual encouraged Joe to go after—do not fit this description. They are usually quite savvy about financial matters. Indeed, rather than being grateful that someone has stepped in to help, they play one agent against another to get the best deal. We recognized that Joe wouldn't do well in such a context. He would do well helping uninsured people.

> 2. I commit myself to meeting a tangible goal for helping them that has a specific deadline, with immediate and significant personal consequences if I fail.

Whatever we came up with for Joe to try, it had to have tangible impact on the people whom he was trying to help and immediate personal consequences for Joe in the event that he failed. As we saw in each of his high-performance stories, Joe dealt with the world in concrete and tangible ways. Abstract benefits and distant payoffs had no appeal for him.

Because Joe faced termination unless his sales improved within months, he didn't have to do anything to activate this step of his pattern in the current situation. Later, as his standing with State Mutual improved, he established target dates for executing sales with each customer and worked out a commission arrangement so that he got proportionally less if he missed the deadline. This kept him on his toes and on pattern.

> 3. I develop a partner relationship with the person or persons who need help, so that they feel they want to work with me toward the same goal.

In each of Joe's stories, he had always established a partner relationship so that the person or persons he was helping felt like they were working with Joe to reach a goal that they had mutually agreed on. In this context, *partnering* meant establishing a trust relationship with the person needing insurance—agreeing together on the insurance goal—before examining specific products or prices. This raised the question, What kind of person would see Joe as a partner and work with him in that way? So much of Joe's personality still reflected his high school dropout background and his lack of a college education that I could see the yawning gulf between him and many professionals. When I pointed this out to him, he agreed. He admitted that he didn't have much rapport with the people with whom he had made contact during his first six months at State Mutual. That explained why he was so unsuccessful at selling to them. He felt uncomfortable even going into their offices.

We spent some time exploring the types of professionals who might have come up the hard way as Joe had and how to reach them. We identified graduates of local law schools, people who practiced law with a working-class clientele, self-made businessmen and businesswomen, and paraprofessionals as people with whom Joe could naturally develop the partner relationship that his pattern called for.

> 4. I and my partners recognize that they are novices who have never before tried to do what we've agreed to do and that I

have enough insights and expertise in the subject to be listened to.

In Joe's stories, this was always true. Even when his expertise wasn't world-class, it significantly surpassed that of his partners. We decided that this step meant that he should work with customers who were essentially novices in buying insurance, not with savvy professionals or large companies having sophisticated legal and purchasing departments. By this point, we had begun to understand that Joe would be successful selling to people who would be grateful for his involvement, people who had never really had a top insurance company salesperson spend any time or effort helping them. Wealthy people and very successful professionals were inundated with proposals from insurance salespeople. It was off pattern for Joe to be just one of many competitors for someone's business. He needed his own niche, one that other insurance salespeople had overlooked or neglected.

5. I make an up-front agreement with my partners about what each of us will contribute to the effort and what each of us expects to get at the end.

Joe operated this way in every high-performance story. There was no hidden agenda. He made a clear quid-pro-quo agreement up front. As we explored the selling approaches that he had tried so far, it was obvious that this was where he was most likely to go off pattern. This was his most difficult step. Joe's helper orientation inclined him to give away his services and expertise in the hope that appreciative clients would then buy insurance from him. For people with different patterns, this might be effective. Many salespeople do create a sense of obligation in a client that works well for them. But that technique was off pattern for Joe—it simply didn't work. And it particularly didn't work when he had to compete with hordes of other insurance agents for business.

Whatever approach we settled on, we knew that Joe should work out specific tit-for-tat agreements with his customers. He should tell them what research, expertise, and service he would provide, what information and assistance he would need from them in order to complete the sale properly, what size of sale would entitle them to his continued assistance, and what they could expect in the way of service if they went with him. Joe winced at the discipline that this would require of him, although he knew it was right. But he recognized, and so did I, that he needed clients who would be grateful for his involvement and pleased that he told them the conditions up front.

> 6. I bring my special expertise to bear on the situation, and my partners show that they trust me and respect my expertise by doing what I suggest.

All Joe's high-performance stories indicated that he did not do well when he had to argue the case for his particular solution to an insurance need. Often, his solutions were good. He was a very competent professional. Taking advantage of a client was so contrary to his values that he wouldn't even consider it. But he wasn't sophisticated or verbally agile enough to hold his own, let alone win, against highly articulate and sophisticated buyers. Whenever he got great results, clients had taken his advice almost without question. We needed to come up with some product or service that would not encourage potential customers to question Joe's advice.

> 7. I arrange for all the support I need for my work with my partners and feel it kick in as things swing into gear.

When Joe did his best work, as his stories demonstrated, he always had the support he needed. Then he could negotiate the best arrangements with customers and not worry about whether he could deliver. Whatever strategy we devised for turning Joe's sales around, it had to include sufficient support from the office team to ensure that Joe wouldn't make promises that he could not keep.

> 8. I stay alert to real opportunities that open up, and as I suggest some risks that can take advantage of them, I get my partners' total agreement, so that we share the responsibility if something goes wrong.

Joe's success was partially due to the thorough explanations that he gave to those whom he was helping, even when they urged him to make the best choices for them. Joe worked with people until they fully accepted the responsibility for the decision *with* him so that they wouldn't turn on him if something went awry. Joe needed to engage people so that they wouldn't feel exposed or at risk by following his advice blindly.

This step was another place in which Joe was likely to go off pattern. His helping tendencies and his superior expertise tempted him to make decisions for his clients. Yet his high-performance examples clearly demonstrated that he did not do this when things worked really well. Rather, he worked with people until they deeply understood what he proposed to do and shared responsibility with him for any risks.

> 9. I follow through thoroughly on everything that I begin and watch the genuine amazement and then gratefulness on the part of the people whom I'm helping as they are treated justly for the first time.

This was another key step in Joe's pattern and another place where he was likely to go off pattern. In his high-performance examples, he followed through flawlessly. Yet in his work for State Mutual, he had fallen down terribly. Quotes that he could have upgraded or sold remained in his files long after the first contact. Insurance follow-up and paperwork can take months to complete, so implementing a good, tight follow-up procedure needed to have top priority in any plan for turning Joe's sales around.

The Key Insight

You may have seen it, but the key insight, of course, was that Joe was trying to sell to the wrong clients and selling products about which he had no special expertise and to which he had no special commitment.

Why the wrong clients? Joe was off pattern trying to become a financial adviser to doctors and lawyers. Such clients didn't need help of the kind that motivated Joe. They weren't disenfranchised nor were they threatened with being taken advantage of. In fact, they might well be the ones taking advantage of little people. Joe needed a clientele that felt more or less powerless and that would be grateful for any help he could give.

I explored with him the types of clients and sales that had really brought him satisfaction over the years, and the stories he told were wonderful. Tears came to his eyes when he described a phone call from a woman who worked on the assembly line in a small (fourteen employees) manufacturing company. The year before, he had persuaded the company president to cover his employees with a disability package. The woman had been slightly injured on the job, enough to cause her to be an outpatient at the local hospital and then to miss four days of work. In the past, she had had to cover most of her losses herself. Now, the policy covered not just her medical expenses but the time lost at work as well.

I asked Joe how he had made the sale, and he said that the company president had been someone like himself, self-made, who had built a little company into something that brought him and his employees a decent living. The president remembered what it had been like to have no insurance and wanted to give his employees some coverage. Joe was able to work out a package that fit the situation. The president was grateful. So were the employees.

The more we talked, the more Joe realized that he was instinctively drawn to poorer, uninsured or underinsured working people and to the small business owners for whom they worked. These were people who needed his services. If he focused on selling disability policies to these people, particularly to small business owners, he would be providing his clients with long-term care and support. Joe knew that he would find great emotional satisfaction in providing service to these people, whom he felt had been shortchanged by the system.

This idea meshed with the expertise aspects of his pattern too. Disability insurance is a particularly complex field. In learning how to insure against actual loss and degrees of disability, and how to broker disability policies, Joe could become (and indeed became) one of a handful of disability experts in his region. He could also become the recognized expert in his office.

Joe even found that he could go back to his days of selling door to door. Many small businesses operated out of a warehouse section in the town. Joe started pounding the pavement there, going door to door, getting in to see the business owner, explaining his product, and selling the owner on the idea. State Mutual had one of the best disability products, and Joe found he had an instant rapport with people like these small businessmen as well as with their working-class employees.

By the end of the year, Joe was one of State Mutual's top insurance salespersons, ranking second in his office. In the six months after we worked with him, his annual sales rose from $12,000 to $400,000. More than that, the satisfaction had returned. He loved what he was selling and to whom. He also had gone contrary to the conventional wisdom of the office and shown the much more sophisticated agents that turning up their noses at selling standard packages had been shortsighted. As Joe's disability expertise increased (and as he began a rapid climb up the chart of total sales for the year), others in his office called on him to expand the proposal that they were putting together by including a disability quote.

Joe became successful by finding his own niche. The insight provided by his pattern gave him the courage and confidence he needed to go in this direction, although everyone in the office thought it was a recipe for failure. Joe flouted conventional wisdom, did what fit him, and succeeded.

General Principles

Some people may view the use of Joe's pattern that I have just sketched as limiting Joe in some way. Yet for Joe it was incredibly releasing. He had been locked into a situation in which his High Performance Pattern had no real chance of operating, so he was attempting to succeed by imitating others and by grinding out some kind of results. Not only was it not working, he was rapidly losing confidence in himself. Learning to take his pattern seriously and finding a way to be true to it—to operate with integrity—turned the situation around.

This solution should not be viewed as suggesting that there was something wrong with Joe because he could not sell well to professionals. At a deep level having to do with his personal values, he didn't want to. He found no satisfaction in selling to people who didn't really need help, nor was winning against other agents who competed for the same business rewarding. Joe found personal meaning in providing expertise and help to people who had usually been overlooked and forgotten.

Some of the saddest cases documented in our files are those of people who, by dint of grinding it out have become "successful" doing something that does not fit deeply held values and that consequently gives them little real satisfaction. Patterns help us to identify the truly rewarding circumstances. When people start using their energy and skill in service of their deeply held values, their lives take on much more meaning. This development is reflected in much higher real-world results.

12

Cutting a Staff to Its Best Performers

THE CASE OF THE TIRED EXECUTIVE FACING YET ANOTHER TURNAROUND SITUATION

That a person is off pattern does not mean that he or she is incompetent. Quite the contrary. Many people do highly competent work in a certain arena for years, enjoying a well-deserved reputation, without being true to their pattern. When this long display of competence has not been particularly satisfying, chances are good that the person accomplished it off pattern. And competence achieved largely by grinding it out eventually takes its toll. Faced with yet another case of needing to be "tough" or "gentle" or to work with a highly charged political situation in the absence of any connection with deep personal meaning, this person begins to rue the day when he or she was first recognized as having this particular kind of expertise.

When you face such a scenario, you need to look at what it would take to kick the situation into overdrive. You need a way of handling the situation that makes it a genuine high-performance experience, not just another task that you grind out competently. Your High Performance Pattern can help you find that right way, the way that gives you a deep sense of meaning and purpose. Then you will be able to combine all the experience and competence that you have amassed over time in facing similar problems and transform a potentially grueling project into an upbeat and deeply rewarding experience.

Patterns contain, and serve to remind people of, all the things that they need to do in order to be deeply successful instead of producing just another acceptable, competent outcome. At best, the pattern pinpoints the key action that will kick the situation into the high-performance realm.

The Case of the Tired Mess Straightener

Marsha Kemp was a tough risk taker who often found herself breaking new ground. She and her husband had three small children when he was a graduate student at Notre Dame. Because she needed to work while he was in school, she helped establish the first university-sponsored day-care center there. After her husband graduated, Marsha went to the University of Southern California, where she earned an M.B.A. Once in the work force, she was promoted quickly. She leapfrogged over many senior people to be named senior market research analyst at Matthews International (MI), a major drug manufacturing firm, where she helped to plan product marketing in the United States and abroad. Later, she became the first female vice president of the company. Being a groundbreaking person was part of who Marsha was.

In her sixth year at Matthews International, Marsha was appointed director of the company's market research group. She was the first woman to hold this key post, in which she evaluated the products that emerged from research and development (R&D) to determine their potential market value before the money was spent to launch them. It was at this juncture in her career that we met Marsha and worked with her to determine her High Performance Pattern.

The market research group was the key filter between MI's marketing and sales divisions and the products flowing out of R&D. Everyone in management agreed that this critical group was not providing adequate service to the company. Marsha was promoted with the expectation that she would shape it up. She had strong senior management support for her task, and her performance would be highly visible. If she succeeded, it would be a real feather in her career cap.

For years, the market research team had been badly managed, and it had underperformed. The staff had acted primarily as data collectors and limited themselves to responding to specific queries from the operations groups. Even at that low-functioning level, they often provided only partial answers to questions, and then often after the deadlines for answers had passed. The group's work and consequent reputation were so pathetic that operations managers and executives had taken to bypassing it and contracting for their own research.

Marsha understood that, to build the research group into a team that would have a significant influence on the marketing of Matthews International's products, she had to work fast to improve both on-time performance and the quality of the research produced. She would have to eliminate from the team any analysts who could not meet these new high standards. There were sixteen analysts in the group. Marsha believed that she would have to fire at least ten of them—maybe more—and bring in new blood.

Bad as this prospect was, it was only one aspect of Marsha's dilemma. She framed her real problem with stark clarity when we started working together: "I have a reputation in the company of being the person to call on when someone has to come in and clean up some messy situation. My style of dealing with people is no-nonsense. Reorganizing the group is old hat for me. I can do it, and I will. But I don't particularly enjoy being the hatchet person. I'm not at all sure that I want to continue doing this. How can knowing my High Performance Pattern help me handle this situation? I already know that I can handle it, but can I really make it a high-performance experience? This kind of task has always been something that I've had to grind out."

So saying, Marsha presented me with the key challenge. Could I take something she knew that she could do but that was unpleasant and use her High Performance Pattern to help her find a way of making it a high-performance experience? Marsha believed that, if she could revamp the department in a way that was upbeat and exciting to her, she would do a much better job. But she also did not believe that that was possible. And having to take on yet another brutal cleanup task was really getting to her.

The key to it, we both agreed, was how she went about weeding out the low performers. One possibility was to use her gut instincts to select the best analysts in the group, eliminate the rest, and bring in her own new people to fill the vacant slots. This was a tried-and-true way of ensuring that she could create an effective, tightly run marketing research group. But there was a basic lack of fairness about it. Marsha didn't like treating people that way. So how could she eliminate the weak analysts in a way that became an upbeat and exciting project for her and the department? How could she avoid the personal toll that her previous grind-it-out successes had exacted from her?

After we found Marsha's High Performance Pattern, we looked at the problem in light of it to see how she could deal with the current situation most effectively. As you will see, she found the key insight that she needed in step 5 of her pattern. The other steps served to ensure that she attended to everything that she needed to do in order to be successful.

As Marsha's pattern illustrates, she needs three major components in order to do her best work: She has to turn a situation around or change its direction, she has to have someone who will back her, and she has to have one leverage point for change behind which she can mass all her efforts. She then builds a strong case for this line of action and forces everyone to get off the fence about it. The result is a strongly aligned team that successfully turns the situation around.

Marsha recognized that, once she removed all but truly top-notch people from her department, she could direct them to produce the necessary top-quality research in a timely manner. That would be the basis on which she could build an influential department. But she had inherited a grab bag of badly managed people, many of whom seemed incapable of work of the caliber that she demanded. It was now up to her to sort them out—to eliminate the truly weak and to assign the capable appropriately.

We discussed how Marsha might do this in a way that fit her. As we began to compare her pattern point by point with the situation, we realized that the first four steps had already been satisfied. She had been asked to bring about a radical change in the direction of an established department (step 1). True to her pattern (step 2), she had initially fought against assuming leadership over the group, but because she trusted her boss (step 3), she had agreed to take on the challenge. She knew that her boss would support her in evaluating the people and eliminating those who were not capable. She had decided that the one part of the activity that she needed to focus on immediately was the quality and timeliness of the work (step 4).

High Performance Pattern
for Marsha Kemp

1. I am asked to, or realize that I must, use my energy to bring about a radical change of direction in an established activity.

2. I initially resist, honestly asking all the right questions and raising all the tough issues, to put the choice in the starkest terms that I can.

3. I find a key person and proceed once I decide I can trust that he or she will back me and that, when push comes to shove, he or she really wants to make a difference.

4. I consolidate my resources and search very carefully for the parts of the activity that I can change to make the new direction take hold and begin to work.

5. I carefully build the case for what I think ought to be done—doing my own research or demanding very high-quality work from my staff—until I believe in it and can present it in a way that protects my reputation.

6. I put everything on the line behind the key leverage point, presenting it as a win for all involved and insisting on support from everyone if needed.

7. I wait while people work through their resistance and then confront them absolutely honestly with the realities of the new situation with which they have to deal until they get off the fence and come aboard.

8. I keep up steady pressure toward the goal, building a tight-knit team in which everyone has a role to play and in which people support one another in working to their personal best.

9. I find that we achieve the goal much more quickly and to a much higher quality than I initially believed possible.

10. I become, much to my surprise, a model for others who regard what I did in retrospect as both brilliant and obvious.

This realization left her confronting the issue of the analysts' quality. If the only way of turning the group's reputation around was by getting it to produce timely, high-caliber output, Marsha would have to eliminate weak analysts—and soon. She feared, naturally, that the majority couldn't make the grade. Before she took the job, she had been acutely aware of the group's reputation and the near-ridicule that it attracted. She knew and disliked on principle the brutal ways of eliminating people that she had seen other specialists in turnaround use. Just as a practical matter, she didn't want equal employment opportunity challenges or wrongful discharge suits on her record if she could avoid them. But she also felt strongly that people deserved a fair chance to prove themselves when a major change was put into place. And this group had been so poorly managed in the past that it might well have real, albeit invisible, strengths. Marsha had the power and backing that she needed. Now she had to determine the right way of handling this people issue.

Step 5 was the key to Marsha's pattern: building the case for a particular change that protected and enhanced her reputation. She knew she could simply assess the people in the department and brutally terminate those whom she didn't think made the grade. But to kick the situation into high performance would require making the case for those to keep and those to let go in a way that enhanced her reputation. Then she wouldn't be doing just another dirty job. She'd be setting another example.

Discussing how to do this, we came up with the idea of giving each of the staff members whom she had inherited a chance to prove him- or herself. That way, Marsha could base her judgments on the quality and timeliness of the work produced, not on anything else. Hard performance data were the best on which to base a decision to let someone go. It would also ensure that the department's ongoing work continued during reorganization. Eliminating two-thirds of the department in a major restructuring would undoubtedly mean a significant lapse in ongoing work until new people had been hired and brought up to speed. But if Marsha followed through on the staff proving themselves, the organization could expect to see a sudden jump in the quality and timeliness of the department's output. People would notice. Marsha resolved to proceed in this way. She would produce a model for reorganizing that might well set a standard for the organization.

Marsha's pattern indicated that she should go ahead with this plan even if her boss or other executives worried that she was not being decisive enough or that she was wasting time. She could defend her plan as a valid, accurate way of sorting through her people. All she wanted from her boss was support in transferring those who didn't make the grade. Marsha's energy level visibly picked up when she began to see the assignment not as a dirty task that someone had to do but as a model for future reorganizations.

We continued to refine the idea until Marsha was really excited about it. We came up with the idea of handing each member of the group a sealed envelope containing an assignment specifically related to enhancing the quality and timeliness of some ongoing departmental project. They would be instructed to complete the assignment by a certain date, despite other demands on their time, and told that they would be judged on the quality of their work. This would be a powerful team-building activity. Individuals would not be competing with one another but demonstrating individually whether they could do work to the new standards.

Marsha acknowledged in meetings with group members that they had not been managed well and expressed her commitment to giving each of them the opportunity to demonstrate his or her ability, thus controlling the outcome.

Marsha expected people to claim that they were so overloaded that they could not find time to complete the assignment. Keeping step 7 of her pattern in mind, Marsha decided to ignore this resistance and confront them with the primary realities of the situation. She needed to be sure that she could count on the quality of her staff's work. Because these test tasks were real, they would help to complete work that the group had to accomplish in any case. Meeting deadlines was a necessary requirement to building a reputation for service. The tasks were neither extra nor optional.

Just as her pattern predicted, when Marsha moved forcefully in this way and kept up the pressure, the analysts rallied in a way that no one had ever seen them do before. They quickly became a tight-knit team working to support one another. Much to her surprise, a number of the people whom her instincts had said couldn't do the work produced exceptional work. She actually had to remove only three of the sixteen. And with the results of their challenge assignments in hand, Marsha encountered no arguments from those whom she dismissed.

After Marsha sifted out the low performers, the remaining staff quickly became an even stronger team. The survivors of the challenge assignments had produced work that truly represented their personal best, and they wanted to become a very high-performing unit. Much sooner than she had imagined, Marsha found that she truly loved managing this group. Her success was highly visible. She had turned a really bad situation around very quickly with much less disruption and nastiness than usually accompanies such a revamping. This was no small factor in her subsequent promotion to vice president.

Marsha was delighted to find that she could turn her department around even more directly and effectively by remaining on pattern than she could if she had used her typical grind-it-out process. Not only was the work less of a grind for her, but she felt much better about her decisions. As her pattern suggested, the challenge assignments became the cornerstone of her turnaround process.

True to her pattern, what she did became a model for other people in the company.

General Principles

Many times, people under the gun to produce quick results believe that they don't have time or cannot take the risk to follow their High Performance Pattern. This is an extraordinarily shortsighted view. In order to do your best work, you must do it in the way that fits you. The more the pressure increases, the more you need to find your best way of doing it. After working through the situation with her pattern as the guide, Marsha was willing to take that risk. She came to believe the underlying idea behind the use of High Performance Patterns: To accomplish a task in the briefest, most solid way possible, make it a high-performance experience. The result was a well-documented and defended decision that worked better than expected and that eliminated painful side effects for Marsha and the company. For the first time in her career, a turnaround assignment had become a truly high-performance experience for Marsha. She no longer feared being saddled with a reputation for being able to straighten out messes. She could now deal with them in ways that didn't drain her. And from the company's point of view, Marsha was something of a miracle worker. She had set an example that others could follow.

Marsha's situation reflects the realities that confront almost any manager or executive who is promoted or transferred to a new assignment. Regardless of how well-run the operation may have been, in order for it to continue to operate at the highest level, the leadership style of the new manager has to take hold in a positive way. High Performance Patterns help to identify the most successful way of leading and to focus attention on specific changes that will actually make it work. There is an obvious premium on not disrupting a group that was well run in the past. But turning around a poorly managed, demoralized group in the least disruptive way possible also has a great advantage. Your High Performance Pattern suggests the least disruptive way of taking charge.

As managers and executives become more confident about using their patterns, they often distribute them to their employees, explain them, and answer questions about them. It helps for employees to know how their boss works best, just as it helps them for the boss to know how they work best. The next step is to find the patterns of all the employees and to engage in a team-building exercise in which the group sees to it that everyone contributes to the collective results in a way that works best for him or her. This is a very powerful route to developing a sustained high-performance team. I will elaborate on it in a forthcoming book.

13

Holding to Strong Values While Executing a Tough Corporate Decision

THE CASE OF THE THIRD-WORLD EXECUTIVE CREATING OPPORTUNITY FOR LAID-OFF EMPLOYEES

High Performance Patterns usually embody deep personal values. It may be unfashionable in some circles to believe that deeply held personal values have any place in business, but the opposite is actually true. High levels of sustainable performance always involve some connection to deeply held personal values. Moreover, since a High Performance Pattern works repeatedly in a wide variety of situations, it has to embody deep personal values. No pattern that describes a person who grabs for short-term, one-sided advantage would work more than once or twice before people found out and effectively cut the person off.

This does not mean that a person can ignore corporate values or pursue his or her own narrow personal values at the expense of others. It means that a High Performance Pattern can often help a person find a line of action that allows the person to remain true to his or her principles while carrying out a corporate directive. This type of solution treats both positions with respect and responds to both with integrity.

Creative Downsizing: Helping the Laid-off Typists

For more than a decade, Tomas Vargas had been an executive of the Latin American operations group of Palmer Corporation, one of the world's largest consumer product companies. A vice president, he headed a staff of one hundred at the company's offices in Bogota, Colombia. His staff included fifty-five salespersons, ten administrators, and thirty-five typists who prepared sales and financial reports and all the office correspondence.

Much to his dismay, he received an order from international headquarters in Miami that the Bogota office was to be computerized. Twenty-five of the thirty-five office typists were to be dismissed.

Tomas knew that, in Colombia's poor economy at the time, the twenty-five typists would have little chance of finding replacement work to support their families. Even if they were trained on Palmer Corporation's new computers before the layoff, their chances for employment were still limited. Palmer Corporation was one of the first companies in Bogota to convert clerical work to computer technology.

How could Tomas use his pattern to make decisions about the layoff in a way that would be fair to the secretaries (one of Tom's deep personal values) and also meet the needs of Palmer Corporation's directors and stockholders?

As Tomas faced the unchangeable circumstance of the layoffs, we began to look at his predicament, step by step, in light of his High Performance Pattern. Tomas had no alternative to terminating the typists, but he hoped to work with them and with his company creatively so that everyone would be treated fairly.

Tomas's pattern indicated that this situation fit him well, despite the frustration that he felt. All his high-performance stories were about situations without alternatives for which he had found solutions that benefited as many people as possible. This was one more situation that required such a creative response.

After we found his pattern, we began to brainstorm and speculate about ideas that might meet everyone's needs. When we reached step 4 in Tomas's pattern, he discovered new ways of looking at the problem and new notions to consider that led to a remarkably creative solution.

Though this process is becoming familiar to you, I must emphasize that we must treat the steps in patterns as neutral facts about a person. I might wish that Tomas were different. Even Tomas might

High Performance Pattern for Tomas Vargas

1. I find myself faced with a situation that is creating fear and desperation for a particular group of people and that seems neither to have a positive solution nor to offer any viable alternatives.

2. I rapidly make the decision to do what I can to resolve the problem myself by finding a solution that will benefit as many people as possible.

3. I obtain as much information as I can from the people affected by asking what would help them if it were possible, giving them a chance to voice their fears to a listener who cares, and building their trust.

4. I identify all the different routes that might shift the negative impact. Then I take the one that will be the best for all concerned, regardless of its precedent-setting nature.

5. I assume the position of leader, with the blessing of those affected, to better drive this progressive change in my own way, and I use my own expertise gently yet effectively to reshape the forces that created the situation in the first place.

6. I personally set the first steps on the route into motion, contacting and getting the right people to act at the right moment to break the seemingly unstoppable movement toward the negative outcome.

7. I use the first results of the work to justify the approach, proving logically to those who resist that this alternative way will bring benefit to all concerned in a way not previously conceived, and they begin to come over to my side.

8. I continually reevaluate earlier steps as I learn more, making corrections to keep the project strong and hopeful while driving it toward completion.

9. I watch the people involved relax, take more and more ownership, and begin to exceed the expected results. This development generates great satisfaction for me and for them while assuring that this new precedent will last.

wish that he were different. But the truth is that he will only do his best work if he can act in a way that is consistent with his pattern. Thus, we both must try to find a line of action that has integrity with his pattern. I asked Tomas if he was on pattern with each pattern step. If he wasn't, we brainstormed until we found a way of acting that would be on pattern for him and still deal with the realities of the situation.

Now let me take each of the items in turn and describe how we looked for creative ideas that could resolve Tomas's dilemma.

> 1. I find myself faced with a situation that is creating fear and desperation for a particular group of people and that seems neither to have a positive solution nor to offer any viable alternatives.

We looked first to see if this situation in fact met the criteria under which Tomas did his best work: fear and desperation for a particular group and no alternatives. He certainly had no alternative to laying off the twenty-five typists. At the same time, he did not see any solutions that could meet the typists' needs. We both felt that the situation fit his pattern perfectly in the sense that it was the type of situation in which he did his best work.

> 2. I rapidly make the decision to do what I can to resolve the problem myself by finding a solution that will benefit as many people as possible.

I asked first whether Tomas had made a decision to get involved and resolve the problem. Indeed, he had. He had already felt that he should handle anything as drastic as laying off twenty-five people personally, so he was involved. However, he had been thinking only about how to minimize the disruptive side effects on Palmer Corporation operations and how to minimize the emotional distress of those laid off. But this step in his pattern states bluntly that, when Tomas does his best work, he thinks about *benefiting* as many people as possible. I pushed him hard on this one. I told him that he'd never come up with a creative solution and a high-performance outcome unless he stopped limiting himself and started asking how to accomplish the larger objective of benefiting as many people as possible.

After thinking about my challenge and reviewing some of his high-performance stories, Tomas agreed with me. He had been thinking about his dilemma on too small a scale. He knew that those who stayed would benefit. The new computers would give Palmer Corporation a competitive edge. To get a truly outstanding result, he had to find some way of benefiting even the typists who were laid off. Tomas decided that he wanted all thirty-five of the Bogota typists, as well as Palmer Corporation's administration and stockholders, to benefit from the introduction of computers. Now the question was how to do that.

3. I obtain as much information as I can from the people affected by asking what would help them if it were possible, giving them a chance to voice their fears to a listener who cares, and building their trust.

Tomas had already interviewed the typists and knew that they all needed continuing work in order to support their families. Many were frightened. Many begged him to let them stay on until they at least were trained on the new computers, believing that that would give them a new marketable skill. Tomas was convinced that computer training would be of limited use to them at that time in the Bogota economy. No other companies were using them.

Again, I pushed him to be true to his pattern. Because it was part of his pattern, I wanted him to take the typists' suggestions for help seriously. Could he provide them with a training program? Was it possible they were more closely in touch with demand in the secretarial field than he was and that training on a new technology would be helpful? Could he be wrong about the number of computers available? Even if there weren't many now, there certainly would be in the future. Computers were the coming technology. Wouldn't training the typists on them at least help?

Tomas replied that he was certain there weren't many computers. Colombian import duties had priced them so high that no one could afford them. Only the largest companies could absorb the cost. "On the other hand," he mused, almost as an aside, "I won't be using ten computer terminals twenty-four hours a day." We looked at each other. This passing glimmer of an idea soon spawned an astonishingly creative solution.

4. I identify all the different routes that might shift the negative impact. Then I take the one that will be the best for all concerned, regardless of its precedent-setting nature.

I pointed out to Tomas that his pattern required him to consider all different routes, no matter how unusual they might be. Once Tomas took the idea of considering alternate routes to solving this problem seriously, he became extremely creative. Even a generous severance package would not help the secretaries feed their families for long. He began to mull over out loud his insight that the company's new computers would be used only during the daytime for years to come.

What if he arranged for all the secretaries to be trained on the company computers and then rented computer time to them, at a low fee, during off-hours, so that they could provide services to Palmer Corporation during busy times as subcontractors? What if the secretaries could then offer their services to other clients in Bogota, renting even more off-hours of computer use; providing a valuable, saleable service; and generating income for Palmer Corporation? The secretaries would not be working for Palmer Corporation, but they would have the makings of a solid cottage industry as computer-literate typists who had access to high-level computers!

Tomas was visibly excited by the idea. He had been depressed about the situation because he had seen no way out. Now he saw a solution that would bring immense benefit to all parties concerned. I carefully pointed out the last part of this step in his pattern. When he did his best work, he took the best alternative, regardless of its precedent-setting nature. I wanted him to trust that it would work in this case, too. If he did this, the corporate people in Miami might get somewhat upset, but if he handled their concerns correctly, he would not only meet the needs of the typists, he would enable them to provide a very valuable service in Bogota—a city woefully short of computers. He smiled and said that he was certain there were ways to make it work.

5. I assume the position of leader, with the blessing of those affected, to better drive this progressive change in my own way, and I use my own expertise gently yet effectively to reshape the forces that created the situation in the first place.

Now that Tomas had an approach in mind, he was ready to drive the situation. He knew that the secretaries would be delighted that he was leading the effort personally. He also thought that if he succeeded here, it would establish a precedent and reshape the forces anyhow.

6. I personally set the first steps on the route into motion, contacting and getting the right people to act at the right moment to break the seemingly unstoppable movement toward the negative outcome.

He knew exactly whom to call, which arguments would be persuasive, and who needed to be influenced by whom. He did not think it would take him long to set it up. I asked him to make lists of the people and what he needed from each so that he wouldn't forget anyone. To my surprise, he didn't think that he was going to have any trouble with anyone on the list.

At this point I knew that Tomas had had the breakthrough that he had been looking for. He had found the key line of action that was true both to the requirements of the current situation and to his own deeply held values that required him to benefit as many people as possible. He had discovered what may have been the only line of action that did both. Once he found it, he wouldn't let it go.

We dealt with the remaining items of his pattern somewhat more superficially. It would be some months before he acted on them, and exactly what he should do would be more clear as that time approached.

7. I use the first results of the work to justify the approach, proving logically to those who resist that this alternative way will bring benefit to all concerned in a way not previously conceived, and they begin to come over to my side.

This step in Tomas's pattern suggested that, when Tomas did his best work, he started small, got some good results, and used those results to convince anyone who resisted that he had handled all the problems. In this specific situation, it meant that, after the first secretaries had been trained and started using the equipment without harm to Palmer Corporation and with the positive benefit of providing the company with rental income, Tomas could use that information to convince others. He was confident that he would persuade the resisters to support his approach.

> 8. I continually reevaluate earlier steps as I learn more, making corrections to keep the project strong and hopeful while driving it toward completion.

This step suggested that, as Tomas implemented his plan, he would learn and make corrections as needed. Among the items that we noted at this time that he needed to learn more about were security issues pertaining to the building and the company's files while nonemployees were using the computers at night and assistance to the typists in setting up their own service companies (licenses, bookkeeping, and so on).

> 9. I watch the people involved relax, take more and more ownership, and begin to exceed the expected results. This development generates great satisfaction for me and for them while assuring that this new precedent will last.

Tomas was certain that, in time, the subcontracting secretaries would come to be a great asset both to Palmer Corporation and to other companies in Bogota. As the program succeeded, he was sure that it would become a model for future layoffs elsewhere in Palmer Corporation as well as elsewhere in Bogota. (As it happened, Tomas got considerable press coverage for the idea, which generated a lot of business for the laid-off typists.) Tomas was now convinced that everyone involved in this unchangeable circumstance could experience great benefit and satisfaction.

Finding the Truly High-Performance Line of Action

Over the years, we have found that there is always a line of action consistent both with the realities of the current situation and with the person's need to be on pattern with integrity. These lines of action produce sustainable high-performance results. If a procedure is inconsistent with someone's High Performance Pattern, he or she will not pursue it with the drive and enthusiasm necessary for sustained high performance. He or she will grind out another acceptable result and be glad when it's over. Of course, if a line of action is inconsistent with the realities of the current situation, it will not work. Only when it fits both the situation and the pattern with integrity will it truly take off.

It takes creativity to discern that fine line of action. There is no algorithm that you can plug a pattern into and have a perfect solution pop out. Nevertheless, your High Performance Pattern functions like a series of signposts, pointing the way to perhaps the only solution that will really work under present circumstances. It is up to us, in managing our own patterns or in working with others, to read those signposts, take them seriously, and see where they lead. Usually, when people are stuck producing merely competent solutions, it is because they are not taking their patterns seriously enough.

A careful review of this chapter will show that I knew nothing about conditions in Bogota and that I was not imposing my own values on Tomas. I just honored what his own pattern said would work best for him and helped him to analyze his situation in light of that. I devote most of my consulting or my training of managers to getting everyone involved to take the patterns as seriously as possible.

When faced with a problem, people commonly assume at the outset that they won't be able to satisfy the demands of their pattern. That was Tomas's assessment at the beginning. His deeply held values surfaced in his thinking only when I confronted him about the meaning of step 2. Those values made him scrutinize the situation far more thoroughly for a course of action. And once he had connected deeply with finding a high-performance solution, absolutely nothing could hold him back. Over and over, I see that people who stay true to their own best way of working and to its suggestions for dealing with a situation arrive at a novel but highly practical line of action that produces results far better than anyone would have thought possible if they had merely followed the conventional wisdom or logic.

Honor your pattern. Honor your best way of working. It is the route to truly creative ways of optimizing the contribution that you can make to almost any endeavor.

14

Giving Something
Your Best Shot
Even If It Doesn't Work

THE CASE OF THE EXPLOITED LESSEE
AND THE INTRACTABLE LANDLORD

Staying on pattern can be very helpful even if the situation doesn't work out as planned. People who approach a conflict with their pattern in mind can feel like they've genuinely given the problem their best shot. Many people waste tremendous energy wishing the past had been different. Using your pattern to guide your actions leaves you with very few regrets, even if it doesn't work. Whether or not a dilemma is resolved perfectly, the person who stays on pattern is more likely to be able to let go and leave the dilemma in the past without lingering guilt or anger.

This chapter presents an example in which the pattern didn't work to resolve a trying problem, at least not in the win-win way that was intended and that many of the other examples in the book illustrate. But because Patricia Rosenberg used her pattern while she was working on her problem, she gave the situation every chance to resolve positively, both for herself and for her difficult landlord. When she ultimately cut her losses and moved on, she was free to leave it behind.

The Case of the Impossible Landlord

Patricia Rosenberg, M.B.A., C.F.P., is director of Rosenberg Associates Financial Planning, author of two books and numerous other publica-

179

tions on financial planning, and a frequent guest on radio and television talk shows. Before she started her own company, Patricia had served as vice president of a large financial planning company for high-net-worth clients and as vice president of an international bank.

Patricia's approach to her clients is personal. She takes their emotional concerns as well as their financial situations into account. She has regular planning sessions with each client and prepares data analyses and creative investment recommendations to meet her clients' needs.

As Patricia Rosenberg's financial planning business grew, she realized that her support services (typing, reception, copying) were inadequate to meet her needs. Her landlord, Roger Atkins, ran his business out of adjacent offices in the building that he owned and provided these services with Patricia's office space rental. Around this time, Patricia discovered that she was paying more than twice as much rent as new tenants for comparable space and services. And Roger's business was declining, so he was reducing his support staff. Not only were his support services inadequate, he was charging Patricia more for the package.

Patricia was furious at Roger when she found this out. She thought the situation was unfair. She was determined to obtain a lower rent and to provide her own secretarial and support services. Yet despite the rightness of her case in her own mind, she found herself unable to begin negotiations to change her situation.

When I asked why, Patricia acknowledged that she felt indebted to Roger—he had taken her on as a tenant when her business was new. She knew from many years of experience with him that Roger was basically closed-minded. She felt that if she confronted him, Roger would insist that the present arrangement was fair, and she was so angry and frustrated that she simply did not want to hear his defense of his position. She was convinced that he would just infuriate her more, and they would get nowhere.

In spite of this, Patricia sympathized with Roger and felt that she owed him something. She hadn't confronted him about the poor service and high rent because she genuinely did not want to make his problems worse. But she recognized that, in taking that position, she was acting as if she were willing to "rescue" him and take it in the

High Performance Pattern
for Patricia Rosenberg

1. I am presented with an opportunity to help someone find a solution to an immediate need, which is in no way incompatible with my own personal interests and values.

2. I see that I have the opportunity to do very well, that I can give a high level of personal consideration and service, and that I can empower the person at the same time.

3. I really listen and observe carefully to get to the root of the need. Before making my diagnosis, I see whether the need expressed is in fact the real need that exists.

4. I put together a structure or roadmap that I'm comfortable will lead to a solution. With it, I find the most appropriate and effective solution.

5. I gently demonstrate to the person in need how my solution can make a difference in his or her situation by staying in touch, letting the person know I'm on his or her side, and presenting hard evidence.

6. I am patient with the process and trust that it will evolve to a place where we can both benefit.

7. I allow the person to work at the pace he or she wants, but I gently nudge the person to keep on track.

8. I respond to crisis situations or roadblocks by staying calm, listening to all facets of the problem, and asking questions until I have all the information and the person has talked himself or herself through to the solution.

9. I get positive feedback from those whom I have helped. I stop, even if only for a moment, to bask in it and feel delighted.

10. I have created a sense of loyalty between us through my high level of personal consideration and service that will carry the relationship into the future.

pocketbook herself rather than confront him on what he was doing and insist that he take responsibility for his own business failures.

Patricia could see that this approach could drag her business down if she didn't change. She also saw that, rather than caring about Roger in an effective way, she was acting as his doormat. If she didn't protest, Roger would never have to acknowledge his own shortcomings and do something about them.

Patricia's way out was to find a line of action that was genuinely empowering to Roger and herself. She needed to make him face up to his commitments in his contract with her. Looking at the situation in this way made Patricia much more willing to be confrontational.

Using Patricia's Pattern

We searched Patricia's High Performance Pattern for specific details of how she should approach Roger and what she should propose. How could Patricia use her pattern to negotiate about her office, without succumbing to quiet guilt or useless anger, and bring the situation to an equitable resolution?

When Patricia focused step by step on her pattern, she found her roadmap for dealing with the problem becoming increasingly clear. By the end of the process, she understood how to proceed without guilt and with a professional and emotional clarity that made it possible for her to end her awkward impasse with Roger.

Now let me take these items one at a time and explain what insights we got and what Patricia eventually did.

1. I am presented with an opportunity to help someone find a solution to an immediate need, which is in no way incompatible with my own personal interests and values.

When Patricia is at her best, this is always how the process starts. She can help someone find a solution to an immediate need, and she doesn't feel compromised.

At first blush, this step does not seem to fit a situation in which Patricia is negotiating to lower the rent that she pays someone whose business is in a tailspin and who needs the money. He is trying to cut expenses and keep his income as high as possible. She wants a lower rent and services commensurate with her growing needs. As Patricia observed, by asking for a lower rent, she would cause an immediate need for Roger. He would need to deal with her demand to pay less rent and her desire to replace his inadequate support services. Rather than helping him find a solution, she would be adding to his problems.

In learning to use patterns as guides, it is important not to reject an approach when your initial take on a situation is that it is incompatible with your pattern. It would have been easy to say that this situation was impossible—off pattern for Patricia—and jump immediately to ways in which she could strengthen her position in what was shaping up as a nasty confrontation.

But it is crucial to treat the pattern as a fact about the person. The fact was that Patricia was more likely to be successful, even in this instance, if she could find a way to approach Roger that let her help him to solve a real, short-term need of his own. It made sense, then, for us not to give up the search for a high-performance solution even when the very first step in Patricia's pattern seemed to show it as impossible. Instead, we asked some more questions. How could she meet Roger's short-term needs. Is there a way? If so, it would work better than confrontation.

There were many ways to approach this situation that would not be high performance for Patricia—threats, compromise, capitulation by one side or the other. She had to find a way to get what she wanted and help Roger at the same time if she wanted a high-performance solution. High-performance resolutions are always in the minority but significantly better when they can be found. A pattern points the way to them.

As I pressed Patricia to meet some of Roger's needs, she saw that she could take over the secretarial and support services for the entire rental space. In return, Roger could lower her rent to bring it in line with the other rents and pay her any small portion of their rents that was applicable to support services. This would relieve Roger of a huge headache and reduce his expenses. Patricia would save enough on her rent to pay the crackerjack support team that she wanted without having to hire duplicate services. Moreover, since she was one of the biggest renters, she knew that providing services for the other tenants (at the reduced level to which their rents entitled them) would not significantly increase the burden on her support team. Details could be negotiated, but the idea made sense.

Patricia felt excited about this way of approaching Roger. It was compatible with her own interests and values, and it would meet a real need of his.

> 2. I see that I have the opportunity to do very well, that I can give a high level of personal consideration and service, and that I can empower the person at the same time.

Patricia knew that she was a much better manager of people than Roger and that she could do very well controlling the support services. She believed she could make a nice profit on just that portion of the business. Furthermore, it would free Roger to improve his marketing of his own business rather than hassling with tenants and support staff. The transfer would empower Roger, in accordance with the second step.

> 3. I really listen and observe carefully to get to the root of the need. Before making my diagnosis, I see whether the need expressed is in fact the real need that exists.

This item suggests that, when Patricia meets with Roger, she should listen closely to his concerns and complaints. She knew that she could not and would not agree with his assessment of the situation, but that was to be expected. If his assessment were correct, his business wouldn't be in such trouble. As she listened to Roger, however, she might find even more insight into his real needs—she could adjust her proposal to serve him more effectively. Most important, she wanted to feel that she really understood Roger's problem from his perspective and, if possible, to have Roger believe that she did. Then she would believe that she had done all she could.

> 4. I put together a structure or roadmap that I'm comfortable will lead to a solution. With it, I find the most appropriate and effective solution.

Since pattern items are sequential, Patricia recognized that she wouldn't know the roadmap's details until after her first meeting with Roger, when she presented her idea and listened to his concerns. However, she was convinced that her proposed service improvement—

and thus her willingness to help Roger with his business situation—was the most appropriate and effective solution. If the negotiations did not work out to her satisfaction, her clear alternative was to find other office space. That move would exacerbate Roger's problems and probably cause him to lose control of the building, but Patricia was now clear that she was justified in that course of action if required. She would not allow Roger's problems to drag her business down.

> 5. I gently demonstrate to the person in need how my solution can make a difference in his or her situation by staying in touch, letting the person know I'm on his or her side, and presenting hard evidence.

Patricia decided that, after the initial exploratory meeting, she would prepare a memo to Roger outlining her situation and proposal and clearly stating how her proposals for improving service in return for rent cuts would meet the needs of both. The memo would fulfill the requirements of this step.

How the First Steps Went

Patricia met with Roger and outlined her basic idea as called for in step 3. It did not go well. Roger categorically refused her proposal. Every effort that she made to get him to talk more about why he opposed it was met with terse answers. She had agreed to pay the rent that she paid, and the support services that he provided were all that he was required to provide. He did acknowledge begrudgingly that he found dealing with support people and tenants a hassle that he'd prefer to avoid, but it came with the territory. The meeting gave Patricia the sense that Roger was in much worse trouble than she had suspected. But rather than either getting angry or feeling too sympathetic, she went right on with the plan that she had based on her pattern. She drew up the letter to him. It presented pro forma budgets to show how the plan would help him as well as herself. She even made the point that he himself would get better secretarial services, since he would use those that she provided. Then she sent it.

I worked closely with Patricia in process as she carried out the rest of the plan. Rather than go into detail, I will touch briefly on the remaining steps in Patricia's pattern.

6. I am patient with the process and trust that it will evolve to a place where we can both benefit.

Patricia was cordial and respectful when she presented her proposal to Roger and discussed it with him. She gave Roger several weeks to consider her offer, hoping that he would come to see its benefits to himself and his own business. Roger was closed and noncommittal during the meeting, but she had fully expected that.

7. I allow the person to work at the pace he or she wants, but I gently nudge the person to keep on track.

After three weeks had passed, Patricia called Roger to request a follow-up meeting. He agreed.

8. I respond to crisis situations or roadblocks by staying calm, listening to all facets of the problem, and asking questions until I have all the information and the person has talked himself or herself through to the solution.

At the follow-up meeting, Patricia remained calm while Roger refused to change either her rent or the support conditions. She questioned Roger until she felt assured that he would not change his position. All her arguments about the benefits to him fell on deaf ears.

At that point Patricia informed Roger that she would begin looking for alternative office space and would give him sixty days notice, as their lease agreement required.

9. I get positive feedback from those whom I have helped. I stop, even if only for a moment, to bask in it and feel delighted.

In this case, Patricia realized that the person whom she had helped was herself. She felt greatly relieved to be out from under the limitations of Roger's rigidity, and she felt "clean" about how she had accomplished it. She had genuinely tried to help Roger, and she was disappointed that he did not see it her way.

Months later, when Patricia saw Roger at the meeting of a professional association, their conversation was cordial. Although Patricia knew that she had not helped Roger improve his business, she had helped him extricate himself from an increasingly awkward situation with her.

In her new space, Patricia saw her business expand and felt delighted that her own needs were being met. Unfortunately, Roger's business situation continued to deteriorate. He eventually lost control of the space and had to move out.

10. I have created a sense of loyalty between us through my high level of personal consideration and service that will carry the relationship into the future.

In retrospect, Roger wished that he had accepted Patricia's offer. It did make business sense. Patricia understood that Roger would never be her fondest ally, but she felt that he bore no ill will toward her that might undermine their work or relationships in the future. She had been as positive and as helpful toward him as she could be, and he recognized that.

Staying on Pattern Helps Even If It Doesn't Work as Expected

Working through this situation, both in planning and in execution, Patricia found that she was most vulnerable to going off pattern during the earliest steps. It was most difficult then to see how she might help someone like Roger find a solution to his immediate need (step 1) when she was the aggrieved person. Then, because she was so angry, she found it hard to listen to Roger to determine his real needs (step 3). She also had difficulty feeling patient with the process (step 6), since money was going out the door, and she wasn't getting the kind of support service that she needed to serve her customers well.

But Patricia could see the value of sticking carefully to her pattern, even if skipping a step or two seemed to promise short-term rewards. By following the process that worked best for her, she genuinely gave it every chance to work both to her own and to Roger's advantage.

When she couldn't reach an agreement with Roger, she was free to leave the situation behind her. Even though Patricia's business has continued to grow and Roger's declined until he lost it, she has not had any feelings of guilt about it. She truly did all that she could.

Following your own pattern not only gives a situation every chance of working out in the very best way. Even if things don't go as you had anticipated, the process leaves you psychologically free.

15

Answers to Typical Questions About Applying Patterns

As I hope you can see from the cases that you have just read, High Performance Patterns structure an interactive process that produces fresh insights about what has or what might go wrong and what you can do about it. The cases in this book involve my interactions, or those of my staff, with the person described. The fact is that the person's manager, coworker, friend, or spouse could have taken my place in the dialogues. The results would have been similar.

Indeed, our program to train people to participate in pattern-based (or mediated) interactions is not particularly lengthy or demanding. Patterns provide so much of the structure necessary for their own use that even people with relatively limited interpersonal skills can make their interactions with others a useful coaching and helping process. Patterns are particularly helpful for managers and supervisors making the transition from directing and controlling people to coaching and supporting them.

As should also be clear, knowing High Performance Patterns does not eliminate the need for hard, creative thinking. Applying your pattern is never a mechanical process. It is a mutual search for the best possible line of action in a complex, messy situation. The pattern focuses attention on your unique qualities, those that make a difference in how well you execute a task. If you can find a way to activate those critical qualities, you will produce better results.

Now that you are familiar with the way patterns work in individual cases, let me summarize some of the principles involved.

Stay True to the Person's Pattern

As I mentioned in the opening section of Part II, one crucial principle is to respect someone's High Performance Pattern, no matter how bizarre it may seem, instead of trying to change it or suggesting that some other way of acting is better than what works for the person. I am continually astonished by the creativity and energy that is released when people experience authentic respect for their ways of working. Most of us fully expect to have suggestions laid on us, and we are armored to resist. We view any time this doesn't happen as a major breakthrough.

Treating the pattern as inviolable is valuable in another way. The most stultifying organizational barrier to creative thinking is the subtle way in which people buy into the way the organization usually does things, thereby failing to see any alternatives. This syndrome militates against creative thinking in any arena. Externally focused problem-solving or planning processes generate very limited options. Sticking to the individual's pattern, which is derived from many kinds of situations, requires fresh ways of thinking. When a step in a person's pattern is unusual and the question is asked, "How on earth would someone go about doing this task in this organization in a way that includes this unusual aspect of this person's pattern?" the blinders come off. New modes of action emerge.

My personal test for the power of any tool is its ability to generate unusual but true insights. Patterns do this with exceptional frequency.

Find the Equivalent of Each Step

For each step in a pattern, you must find a corresponding action step in the actual target situation. Because each situation is different, each exact expression of the action will vary. The creative thinking process requires us to develop analogies. What action step can I take in this situation that is equivalent or analogous (but not identical) to what I did in my past high-performance experiences?

Decide Yes or No and Turn Each No into a Yes

When we compare a pattern point by point with the related actions, we ask the person to respond *yes* or *no* to the question, "Have you done this step?" or "Have you planned a way of doing this step?" Then we focus the discussion on turning *no* answers into *yes* ones. By the end, the person should have developed a line of action that is consistent with the entire pattern.

Although I haven't included an illustration of it in this book, we have developed a way of breaking each pattern step into its implied or embedded yes/no questions. To make application easier, we sometimes give the client this checklist version of his pattern. He thinks it through and then takes any action in the situation that allows him to check yes to each question. As long as he can keep answering yes with integrity to each query, he's on pattern.

Find Unique Twists That Reflect the Individual

When finding a way to do a task that fits your pattern, you can't be satisfied with any action that only approximates the pattern step. When a line of action really fits you, the way in which you accomplish each step has a unique twist that captures your unique way of doing things. I always work with a client until we find that unique twist. Then we know it is truly the person's best way of working.

Take the Initiative to Act

The best planning or problem-solving process in the world is worthless unless we actually take the actions that we have identified. Pattern-based thinking usually results in a specific action that is well tailored to the person and situation and that has a high likelihood of working. Even so, people can always find reasons to avoid taking the action if they wish. Patterns show the route to greater effectiveness. They don't achieve that goal by themselves. In organization and team settings where there is mutual support and encouragement for people to stay on their own pattern, it is much harder for people to avoid action. In many situations, some support system is very helpful.

Keep the Person in Control

We are convinced that the only way in which organizations or teams can ever become high performing is by empowering the individuals in them. For that reason, we explicitly give each client the final say as to what will or will not work. We can never know better than the person who is being helped what is right for him or her. Many other systems depend on experts to interpret what a person should do. These systems often end up having experts decide what's good for someone else. Our principle is to keep the person in control.

Make the Business Case for Better Results

To apply his or her pattern effectively, a person must be able to make a powerful business case for any adaptations that will enhance his or her work. The person's best way of working is a means to getting much better results. Ultimately, the person needs to be able to tell the boss or organization, with conviction, "If I can do it this way, I can deliver this improvement in outcomes." Even the most hard-nosed boss or penny-pinching organization is impressed by an unusual approach that promises to improve results.

Let me now turn to some typical questions about applying patterns.

1. *Doesn't being true to my pattern necessarily mean that others can't be true to theirs? This seems like an extraordinarily selfish way to behave.*

It seems like it is, but it isn't. We do everything that we can to avoid reaching solutions at the expense of someone else or of the organization. Such lines of action do not produce high-performance results, nor are they sustainable. If the person in charge has the power, such a solution can be imposed. But the result is predictably mediocre. High performance always stems from a line of action that merges the participating individual's unique qualities with relevant situational constraints. Then and only then is an outstanding outcome possible. This principle resembles the way in which football teams devise game plans that conform to football's rules, making maximum use of their players' individual strengths in order to counter the strengths of their opponent and ultimately win.

High Performance Patterns make the true strengths of the individual members of a team or organization easy to see, discuss, and meld into a coherent plan. The plan itself must include accurate knowledge of situational constraints (rules, laws, timelines, available money, and so forth) and, if relevant, what competitors are doing. Most organizations already incorporate these considerations into their decision making. What organizations do not tend to consider is individual success processes. At best, when assembling teams, they apply some knowledge of each participant's skills and past experiences.

Our experience suggests that, if people are true to themselves, they actually open up space for others to be true to themselves. Once people start to acknowledge the detail and uniqueness represented by High Performance Patterns in their interactions, they realize that direct conflict becomes very rare. People can usually see various non-conflicting ways of collaborating to achieve a collective result. They also begin to see lots of ways of complementing one another. In the rare instances of direct conflict, two people can almost always reach an agreement that settles things for the time being. Conflict seems huge and intractable only when individuals who know little about one another are forced to relate either blindly or in terms of generalized group characteristics. Digging deeper into the available individual differences and strengths makes it easier to discern ways through apparent conflicts.

2. *Does a pattern change, evolve, and grow? I'm afraid I'll find my pattern and then be locked into it both by my own thinking and by that of my boss and colleagues.*

Yes, a pattern does change, evolve, and grow as the individual gets more experience using it. And yet, while people get better at doing an increasingly wide range of things in a way that fits them, the pattern always remains consistent. The way in which a pattern develops never alters the fundamental way in which the person is successful in the world. It reflects organic changes that extend and elaborate on the original pattern, not deliberate and willful efforts to change in order to be successful in a very different way.

We know this because finding the pattern in the first place involves selecting high-performance examples from different times in a person's life. We ask people who derive their pattern from three relatively recent experiences to test it against some much earlier example in their lives. They universally come away surprised that the basic elements of their pattern were present as many as twenty or thirty years earlier.

A significant number of people take our program twice—typically five to ten years apart—and many others have periodic updates of their patterns every couple of years or so. With these people, we do see growth and development. The pattern becomes richer and fuller. Occasionally a step is broken into two steps because the exact sequence has become more obvious. Yet the people themselves realize that the basic pattern has remained the same. They have just become more discriminating in their ability to understand and apply it.

We also have innumerable people who, either by choice or because their organization imposes some standard practice on everyone, have spent a lot of time learning to do something that doesn't fit them well. When these people know their pattern, they work at making the standard practice into something they can use effectively, using their pattern to move from grind-it-out to high-performance mode and thereby boosting their capability from merely competent to outstanding. When the standard practice is significantly at cross-purposes with their pattern, they select from among its techniques whatever they can really use. In contrast, when people in such a situation do not yet know their pattern, they often get bogged down, learning the new standard practice by rote and trying to apply it mechanically, with little real success or enthusiasm.

You have to make something your own if you want to get good at it. Patterns help in the assimilation process. If people don't use their patterns and don't develop individual variations when they implement a standard practice, most will not make good use of the technique. Ask any experienced manager how successful the implementation of some across-the-board technique was in improving the performance of employees. The usual rule of thumb is about 20 percent. In our view, these are the people for whom the new technique happened to be pretty consistent with their ingrained way of succeeding.

3. *How do High Performance Patterns differ from other approaches to peak performance?*

There is a fundamental difference between peak performance and sustained high performance. Peak performance means cranking one-self up for extreme output, typically over a short period of time. By definition, it is not sustainable. Athletes use visualizations, exercise routines, and diet changes to peak for particular events, such as the Olympics or world championships. Lawyers get themselves up for a particular trial presentation, students stay up all night to cram for an exam, and businesses of all kinds pull out all the stops to meet contract deadlines. However, if any of them attempt to repeat this tactic without significant recovery cycles, they will most certainly burn out rapidly. Witness the drop in performance and the number of injuries toward the end of a summer of athletic competition in Europe, for example.

Although I am aware both that there are many books on athletic techniques and that many consultants make use of them, I am skeptical of any systematic application of athletic techniques to business. My doctoral dissertation dealt with games and simulations, and athletic contests present a much more simplified reality than any business situation. Most important, athletic rules are very clearly established and vastly reduce the range of behaviors possible in any given event. Business situations are never so clear-cut. And competitive advantage can often be gained by inventing radically divergent approaches. Thus, techniques designed for developing strategy and tactics in games have limited utility in the real world, and those for motivating players (or for helping players motivate themselves) have limited utility when goals and tactics are less proscribed.

This is not to deny, however, that many people have found athletic performance-improvement techniques useful or even powerful. They have found something that fits them, and by all means they should continue to use it. However, in our experience, such examples mean simply that someone has found a technique that reinforces an important aspect of his High Performance Pattern. If athletic techniques fit you, great. If they don't, they probably aren't worth your effort.

Probably the most widespread technique for peaking is neuro-linguistic programming (NLP), in which people deliberately recall situations in which they did well that resemble the one they are approaching. They recall past similar successes in great detail and then attempt to repeat whatever they did that worked. This technique is powerful. It is even analogous to High Performance Patterns, except that it works only for very short-term situations. NLP doesn't attempt to look at patterns over many days, months, or years. Also, since its focus is so short-term, the methodology is more manipulative. Rather than finding the authentic route to deep expression of oneself in a situation, neurolinguistic programming promotes the deliberate manipulation of the situation for personal advantage.

4. *I agree that the use of patterns is powerful, but it seems to take a long time. Can busy managers and employees really take the time to use them?*

True, it takes time up front to find the pattern. But after that, since patterns are fundamentally stable and since they grow and develop only in consistent ways over extended periods of time, they can be used over and over again. The initial cost is an investment in the employee. If you are not an employee, the initial cost is an investment in yourself and in your potential for achievement.

Once patterns are known, the speed with which insights can be generated for problem solving is remarkable. This advantage quickly pays for the initial investment. One senior IBM manager told us that, before he knew his people's patterns, a typical problem-solving session took several hours. By the time a problem was significant enough for him to know that it existed, it would take a couple of hours' discussion before he and the person involved really knew what the problem entailed. Once they had a grasp of the situation, it would often take another hour or more before they had worked up a viable solution.

But once he knew his team's patterns, he could cut this time in half, at the very least. The pattern illuminated exactly where something was wrong, reducing the problem-identification task to twenty minutes or so. Figuring out how to get back on track creatively usually took another half-hour or so. Our client found that he was so much more efficient that the original cost of finding the patterns was easily recovered in his time alone. The improved individual effectiveness of his team was all gravy.

It is hard, of course, to calculate the costs of bad decisions and attempts to correct things that don't work. Trial-and-error problem solving is very expensive in both time and morale. Patterns focus attention so quickly and clearly on what the problem is and provide such deep insights that misguided decisions are far less likely when patterns are used. Deciding that there isn't time to use patterns before you start often means finding the time to redo something later.

5. Can patterns be faked?

When I addressed this question at the end of Part I, I pointed out the methodological difficulty in having someone invent consistent stories that presented a picture diverging from truth. Now you have read the case studies. What do you think? Could someone fake a pattern? Even more, now that you understand how patterns are derived and what they do, does it make any sense to fake one? The ultimate proof that a pattern is valid is that it works in some real problem or situation that you are facing. If the pattern isn't true, the action steps won't work. Reality is the ultimate validator.

PART III

Applying Patterns to Pairs of People

One limitation of management literature is that it pays relatively little attention to improving the working relationships between pairs of people. Individuals at various levels of the organizational hierarchy get significant attention. Teams have attracted lots of study, and organizations as a whole are a principal focus. But pairs of individuals have been relatively neglected.

This is ironic, because in the real world of work, getting pairs of people to work together more effectively is one of the most important ways in which results can be improved significantly. Relationships between managers and subordinates are the source of most worker satisfaction or dissatisfaction. The vast majority of people who quit their jobs cite problems with their managers as the primary reason. Although the manager's role as mentor or coach has received a good deal of attention, relatively few researchers have explored the relationship between manager and subordinate as one in which both parties are responsible for making the relationship work. Peer-peer relationships are just as crucial. Tensions between two people on a team or in a department can be highly disruptive for the operation as a whole. And people who operate the interface between two parts of a company—for example, production and warehousing—often have to work effectively together for orders to be filled correctly. Problems between people in these key interface positions can be devastating.

We have found that High Performance Patterns help pairs of people who are having trouble by pinpointing specific changes they can make in the way they work together. The simple language of patterns makes discussing the problem easy. When each person understands the other's best way of working, it is usually a relatively quick process for the two parties to work out a way of handling their conflict.

High Performance Patterns are uniquely powerful for conflict resolution. But they are far more than that. When we use the information that they contain to combine working partners, they have more capacity than any other tool that we know of to enhance organizational effectiveness. Matching managers with subordinates who have complementary patterns can increase their collective effectiveness in achieving overall goals. Peer pairing is an even more neglected area of study, yet in many work situations we have found that deliberate pairing is far more powerful than finding the one right person to do a specific job. A single individual rarely has all the skills, knowledge, experience, or style characteristics needed to deal effectively with some problem or opportunity, but the proper combination of two individuals often does. Patterns facilitate the pairing and help people who don't know each other to quickly determine how to work together.

Patterns are also effective in sorting out what has gone wrong when a long and productive relationship turns sour. Such an application is beyond the scope of this book, but I can tell you briefly that we have found it possible to develop a High Performance Pattern for any relationship that has a long enough history. It is possible to ask, How does this relationship work when it works well? Then, in a manner analogous to that in which we use patterns with individuals, the partners can look at how they have drifted away from what works for them.

We follow a loose structure when we work with pairs of people or train managers or team members to work with pairs:

1. *Read and Discuss Each Other's Pattern.* We work with each person to find his or her High Performance Pattern. Then we bring them together and have them read and discuss each other's pattern. Usually we have both persons share at least one story on which their patterns are based so each party appreciates the rich detail about what works

best. One of our consultants is present at first to help interpret the patterns. When patterns are particularly unusual or unique, we sometimes prepare some summary statements about each person's special strengths, ways of relating to others, and kinds of support and rewards needed to make sure that the patterns are well understood.

2. *Look for Areas of Agreement.* Next, we have the two parties look for areas of agreement—what we call overlap—between their individual patterns. What are they both good at? What similarities are there in the ways they succeed? In particular, what values do they share? People who are at loggerheads often find that they share common values but act on them in radically different ways. Shared values make resolving their conflict much easier. This phase is completed successfully when the two grasp their shared basis for working together.

3. *Look for Areas of Complementarity.* Once the two have identified significant areas of agreement, they look for things that one does which could enhance what the other does. We have them focus on complementary strengths for getting the job done synergistically. They can usually identify some ways in which they can produce better results than each one acting alone. For example, one may be very good at convincing people about something, while the other is very good at handling and neutralizing any remaining resistance. These two can marshal support much more readily as a pair than either could alone.

4. *Identify Areas of Potential Conflict.* Only at this point do we have the pair deal with their conflict. Each person begins by trying to state the conflict from the other's point of view. Then they work on ways of resolving the conflict for the current activity. For truly intractable conflicts, we insist at a minimum that they divide the current activity in half. Wherever they draw the line, it has to be a clean one. However, more often than not, pairs find a positive way of handling the conflict that respects each individual's way of working.

For interpersonal conflicts, we do not believe that it is necessary to find a resolution that will last for all times and all places. In most working situations, our objective is to find a resolution that will work for the duration of the current activity. Even in the rare instances in which the conflict between two people's patterns is truly fundamental—such cases are extremely rare; patterns are too different for fundamental conflict to arise very often—people can agree on a way to handle their conflict for the time being and for the good of the current activity.

5. *State Understandings of How Each Will Operate.* At the end of the process, we always make certain that each person states his or her agreements and expectations to the other party and even writes them down if necessary. This step assures that they have agreed on how to handle the conflict. If there is any misunderstanding about the outcome of the process that has just been conducted, it will show up here.

The Case Examples

The cases that follow are only three of many possible instances. In contrast to the very systematic, point-by-point comparison that we make of a person's pattern in a problematic situation, we use a much more fluid process when we work with pairs. The only exception to this rule is when the pair is really new to one another. Then we go step by step.

- Chapter 16 involves resolving a difficult interpersonal problem between the grandson of the founder of a bank, who expected to be named CEO but was passed over, and the person whom the bank's board installed in his place.

- Chapter 17 describes two managers who used their patterns to come up with a radical restructuring of how they ran a manufacturing plant. The restructuring enabled their strengths to have much more impact in the plant as a whole and eliminated the tension between them.

- Chapter 18 shows how a university president used his knowledge of High Performance Patterns to interview the university board members, determine their High Performance Patterns, and then work out assignments for them that applied their strengths to meeting the university's needs.

16

Finding a New Way of Working with a Colleague in a Difficult Situation

THE CASE OF THE CEO AND THE FOUNDER'S GRANDSON

In our experience, conflicts between people in business situations tend to occur when each person unconsciously assumes that the other person should want to do things their way. We sometimes refer to this as the you-should-do-things-the-way-that-works-best-for-me syndrome.

Because High Performance Patterns are simple, natural-language ways of writing down each person's best ways of working, they help people to discuss these unconscious presumptions. Usually, when a person really understands the other person's way of working and realizes what the other person needs to produce the best results, he or she finds ways of carving up the work that take advantage of the differences. The alternatives—wishing that the other person were different or trying to make the other person change—are usually not effective.

When two people learn their High Performance Patterns, they can find the most effective way of working together. Patterns often provide insights into work dynamics and indicate ways of making business relationships more constructive.

The case in this chapter illustrates that point. Two executives in a very successful bank, one the chairman of the board and grandson of the founder, the other the president and CEO, were having great difficulty understanding each other and determining how to work together effectively for the greater benefit of the bank. Through their patterns, they grasped the nature of their conflict and worked out a resolution.

The Case of the Family-Owned Bank

Alex Field was the oldest son of the third generation of the family that owned Commerce Bank. As the founder's grandson, he had grown up identifying with the bank. When his father died, he expected to inherit the controlling share of stock. He had trained at a major commercial bank and in the bond business, and had held a variety of management positions at Commerce Bank. By all rights, he had expected to direct Commerce Bank as its CEO.

But because his father kept such a tight rein on Commerce Bank's management, Alex had not often been able to undertake his own projects or to make his own mistakes. After his father died, Alex had temporarily become head of the bank, but things had soured quickly. Budgets ran out of control, and revenue dropped. His cousins orchestrated a takeover battle and lost, but in the process destroyed the family control of voting shares. The board and senior bank management selected a new president and CEO to manage bank operations, Mark Hardy. Alex was named chairman of the board and given a limited budget, limited duties, and a small staff.

Mark Hardy was a highly motivated career banker who had been a Commerce Bank executive for a decade. Earlier in his career, Mark had been tremendously successful in fast-moving investment banking and in managing an international development bank. At Commerce Bank, Mark set high goals for efficiency and customer service and soon compiled a distinguished record. As president and CEO, Mark quickly got things under control, increased revenue, and started planning a significant bank expansion program. Few could argue with the board's selection of Mark to direct bank operations.

Alex was chairman of the board, but the board had voted against him in selecting Mark and in giving Mark the real power to run the bank. Alex's only hope for making an impact—for contributing significantly to the bank's future operations—was to develop a good working relationship with Mark. But their working relationship was strained by definition.

Mark was doing an excellent job of running the bank. His success kept a very solid majority of the board behind him. But Mark was uncomfortably overextended in his new position as CEO, and he needed to delegate some of his responsibilities. That meant that he was open to considering an allocation of duties and complementary responsibilities with Alex.

When we began to work with Commerce Bank, our first task was to divide bank responsibilities for Alex and Mark. But I had a deeper goal. I wanted to get to the bottom of the tension between the two men so that a resolution between them would be neither temporary nor superficial.

I started by finding each man's individual High Performance Pattern. Not surprisingly, their patterns were almost entirely different. I saw this as a good sign, because it meant that there was a strong possibility of developing real complementarity between them. They were so different that it should be possible to divide up the various duties involved in heading the bank and carry them out without getting in each other's way or treading on each other's turf.

How could Alex and Mark renegotiate their work responsibilities in a way that accepted and took advantage of each other's dissimilar ways of being successful? How could they work together without undermining the other's efforts?

Here is what I found and what Alex and Mark did to improve their working relationship as a result of my recommendations.

Alex Field's High Performance Pattern

Alex Field had grown up in the upper crust of society in the bank's community. Genial and well-connected socially, his pattern indicates that he would do well directing special projects aimed at maintaining the values and traditions of the bank. When Alex is on pattern, the result is exquisite, a "gem." It is well worth it to have Alex work on pattern. The paragraphs that follow sketch the conditions that Alex's pattern revealed had to be in place if he was to be at his very best.

Alex can produce gems for Commerce Bank if he is "tapped" for special assignments, given the opportunity to build personal "team-like" relationships, and freed from outside pressures.

In each of his high-performance stories, Alex had been asked, invited, or talked into taking something on and eventually persuaded that he was the best person for the job. "I'm not good where I'm not wanted," Alex explained, and indeed he wasn't. In his personal style, he was amiable and good-natured, more inclined to smooth feathers than to ruffle them. Alex would not excel in situations calling for confrontation, although he could hold his own if he had to. In a characteristic way, he chose not to try to fight the board when it elevated Mark to president and CEO. Even if he could have won, he would have not chosen to go where he was not wanted.

In each of Alex's high-performance examples, he had a concrete project with inherent constraints, such as budgets, time lines, or specifications, but no methodological requirements imposed from the outside. As the person in charge of the project, Alex could determine its direction, using outside expertise only when he chose to. Attempting to do what others thought good almost never produced a high-performance outcome for him. It did not surprise me that Alex's high-performance examples invariably entailed doing things his own way.

Alex had a strong sense of tradition that told him what was right in a given situation, and he respected that sense. Although he could get along with anyone, he did not produce his best work in new situations that went beyond his experience base. He needed to assemble a circle of trusted people with very original ideas with whom he could work as a team. He had extensive social and professional connections. When he had prior experience with people, he could maximize their skills without the often rocky and confrontational period of testing. In optimal situations, the people on Alex's team trusted him, and he trusted them.

It was an extremely strong point in Alex's pattern that he enabled each participant to feel capable of contributing to the current project. He was willing to try any idea that might enhance the project. He would often make such decisions on the spot. Needless to say, people liked working for him on a project. The possibility of having an impact was so immediate.

Alex isolated "manipulators" so they could not derail his best efforts by undermining his participatory management style. In his high performance examples, once Alex had identified manipulators who

High Performance Pattern
for Alex Field

1. I am tapped for an assignment to carry out a specific project that has deadlines and a clear outcome because I am the logical choice and well qualified to do the job.

2. I work free of expectations and outside pressure to do the project in any way except my own. The only constraint is meeting the inherent requirements of the activity, such as the deadline.

3. I know, based on experience and a sense of tradition, what is needed in the situation, and I set out to achieve it, even if it is different from what those who tapped me may have in mind.

4. I select the brightest, most able people in my circle of relationships to work with me on the assignment, people with whom I have a past history of trust and respect, to minimize interpersonal difficulties.

5. I develop personal, teamlike relationships with everyone involved to maximize the number of good ideas I have available, making all feel that their idea for making the project better will get a fair chance to work.

6. I insulate myself from manipulators who may try to take the project over by placing my trusted teammates between them and me and thereby keeping myself and the team in control.

7. I continually shape and refine the initial conception as I go along, even to the point of throwing out what has been done and starting over if it does not reach the high standard that I have envisioned for the final product.

8. I rely on my innate sense of quality to know when the final product meets my standards, and I don't stop until I have achieved it.

9. I produce a gem that more than makes up for the initial struggle. Everyone involved in the effort and everyone who sees the product agrees that it is very fine.

wanted to drive a project of his in their own way, he insulated himself from them as quickly and totally as possible by placing his friends between him and them. If Alex tried to fight back against manipulators, he was not particularly effective. Because he was not confrontational by nature, he would have to fight them on their own terms.

Like an artist, Alex constantly evaluated what had been done. During this phase, Alex was very hands on. He compared what had been achieved with his original conception and reworked as necessary. This aspect of Alex's pattern can play havoc with deadlines and budgets, which is why he worked best on projects that had these inherent constraints.

Finally, however, the result of Alex's work was a "gem" that everyone acknowledged as such.

Mark Hardy's Pattern

Mark's pattern showed that he had a special ability to identify the potential in existing structures for much better results. He could spot unused capacity and expand its use without wasted effort. He could see opportunities where others could not.

Mark's best work occurred when he spotted such an opportunity, established specific performance goals early on, and set up a system to monitor the results closely on a daily basis. He worked with a small, loosely structured group of highly competent experts with whom he met on an as-needed basis. Then, as his group got some powerful movement going, Mark let other people "come around," incorporating them and their ideas into the overall effort until everyone was pulling together. Mark loved throwing himself into what he was doing in order to make the situation work really well. As long as things were going well, he could be happy if the work lasted forever.

Two Different Patterns Create an Opening for Complementarity

What could I tell from these patterns about how the two men should work together in order to be at their best? I will explain first how knowing their patterns helped me to understand the specific agreements that they needed to reach and then what happened when I

High Performance Pattern
for Mark Hardy

1. I find a structured situation that permits a lot of growth and that has a lot of unused capacity that either no one else sees or no one else knows how to use.

2. I carefully examine the situation and get involved only if I am sure I can make it work much better and that I can handle it.

3. I create a monitoring system so that I will know how well I am doing at all times as I put things to get the situation moving into place.

4. I select a small group of highly competent experts, give each his or her own area of responsibility, and work with them one on one as needed to achieve common ends in a loosely structured way.

5. I create a schedule of daily activities that is constantly different and challenging, although the basic task remains the same: doing each single activity absolutely as well as I can.

6. I throw myself totally into the job and enjoy what I am doing tremendously, often wishing it could go on forever.

7. I let others who are not part of my small core group get involved at a level they can handle and wait for them to come around if they have been resisting the direction in which I'm moving, incorporating them in as soon as they do.

8. I leave sufficient room to take and run with new ideas, and I encourage others to do likewise, collectively finding ways to maximize the potential of the situation.

9. I watch as the situation begins to maximize its potential, and everyone pulls as hard as he or she can to achieve the common goal, proud to be part of my team.

10. I continue to push the situation until some new one with unexploited potential comes into my awareness.

brought them together to learn about each other's patterns and develop a better way of working together. Their patterns helped me as their consultant, but the process that I used shows how knowing the patterns will help anyone, particularly managers, to improve the working relationship between two people. What I did as their consultant does not differ in principle from what any manager does when two subordinates have ineffective working relationships.

What I Could Tell from Their Patterns

First, my reasoning: I acknowledged the realities of the situation. Mark was in charge. His pattern was the governing one. No solution was possible without his complete agreement. The quest was to find a way in which Alex and Mark could work together that fit them both. Neither should have to compromise his best way of working, and the solution had to have Mark's complete support.

Because I took this primary requirement seriously, I knew that an effective working relationship between these two depended on having Mark select Alex as one of the "experts" whom he needed to run some aspects of Commerce Bank operations. I needed to explore this first with Mark. Did Alex possess some type of expertise that Mark really needed? Was Mark willing to give Alex responsibility for any bank operations requiring that expertise? I was optimistic that such an arena existed, since their patterns were so different.

Assuming that I could pinpoint such an arena, Mark could then set up the hard measures of success that his own pattern required, which included budget and timetable. Then Mark could measure Alex on how well he delivered. This approach would also fit Alex's pattern. He would have autonomy in his areas of responsibility, but he would also have the kinds of built-in constraints that he needed. According to his pattern, Alex needed to be "persuaded" that he was the best person for the job. I would be sure that Mark was really in agreement if he persuaded Alex to take over the operations that he was giving him. This would satisfy both men's patterns. Mark would consider Alex part of his elite team of experts, and Alex would get the initial affirmation that he needed in order to excel.

The next major issue was how Alex could fit into Mark's way of working with his elite team. Mark worked best when he worked alone, and he liked to have his "experts" work alone also. Team meetings were anathema to him. This requirement clashed with Alex's strength: leading a group. Alex liked participatory management and loved the human interaction of teams. We would also have to find a way to accommodate the fact that Alex was project oriented and that he preferred to deliver a particular thing against a deadline and budget, while Mark loved managing an ongoing process and continually making it better.

Even here I was optimistic. Alex liked it best when no one interfered with his way of leading. Mark would not interfere if Alex was delivering. Alex could have his own staff and lead them in a highly participatory way. He would have trouble only in that Mark would not manage him in that way.

Identifying Specific Work Assignments for Alex and Mark

Many of the responsibilities of running a bank involve maintaining and continuously improving ongoing processes. Mark was the obvious person for these. However, many other responsibilities have a project quality. Some set of activities must be engaged in for a relatively short time in order to produce a final event or result. These responsibilities were logical for Alex. And there was another potential split of responsibilities. Bank leaders, particularly the leaders of a local bank, were under pressure to attend the meetings of community groups, participate on community boards, and support local charities. These did not fit Mark at all, but they were natural for Alex's personality and history of connection with the community. The same was true at state and national levels. Attendance at industry meetings, not to mention meetings with various government agencies, was almost a requirement. Mark hated meetings, particularly ceremonial ones. Alex was at home in them.

Working with the Two of Them Together

Armed with these insights and at least two possible ways of dividing responsibilities, I brought the two of them together. I began by having each explain his pattern to the other. They found this very useful.

They discussed aspects of each other's patterns and asked questions about them.

Alex and Mark both had real difficulty understanding the other's preferences. Mark's lack of enthusiasm for teams perplexed Alex, and Alex's project and people orientation puzzled Mark, who preferred to have experts do ongoing jobs well. However, once they understood that each got his best results in the pattern that worked for him, they began to see how both patterns were at once highly effective and complementary.

After they were familiar with the salient points of the other's pattern, I proposed the project versus ongoing division of assignments. Mark liked the idea. He was delighted to turn over a substantial set of projects to Alex: those involving short-term training and various marketing campaigns. Mark hated the relatively short-term nature of these projects. Once Alex had clear responsibility for a set of projects, he loved the freedom to do them his own way. It suited him fine to interact only periodically and one on one with Mark about the project's results and not to have to worry otherwise. So Alex assumed responsibility for short-term training and marketing projects. With his knowledge of the community, he was sensitive to products and promotions that would increase the bank's business. He was also the logical person to direct in-house training programs, since he represented the values of the family that had built the bank.

When I raised the representing-the-bank set of responsibilities, Mark was again delighted with the idea, and so was Alex. It was easy to convince Alex that it would suit him to represent Commerce Bank's traditions and values as a member of community organizations and the local and national banking committees. He genuinely liked these groups, and his experience and sense of tradition told him what would be needed. Most of these groups involved short-term projects and highly interactive work on committees and task forces. Alex would be right in his element.

Mark and Alex now understood how to match each other with responsibilities and began to brainstorm other possible areas. For example, someone needed to oversee the building of new branch offices that would reflect the bank's public image. Alex had successfully developed a new Commerce Bank branch that won accolades (and deposits) from the surrounding community. New ones were a natural for him. Someone also needed to develop strategies aimed at opening new territories for Commerce Bank. Particularly in nearby communities, Alex understood the psychology and market needs that new Commerce Bank branches would need to meet.

Restructuring Mark's Responsibilities

Mark, of course, maintained overall responsibility for bank operations. However, because he now understood how the process worked, he set himself a new challenge. He wanted to restructure his own responsibilities so that he would have more uninterrupted work time and fewer meetings. Mark sought to keep the bank on track in its growth with no surprises. He had established computerized monitoring systems for Commerce Bank that permitted him to track performance. His absolute first priority was staying on top of that. Here were the ideas he came up with.

1. Mark decided that he could consolidate some of the time he spent meeting with bank employees by devoting an hour or two each week to staff interactions. Mark's assistant could schedule people for five or ten minutes each during Bring Your Good Ideas to the President hours. His assistant could also help employees prepare brief memos about their concerns, which Mark could scan before the meeting to conserve time.

Mark considered people who just wanted to chat about an idea or get his approval on something that was clearly within their authority as terrible time wasters. His pattern substantiated his view. With the Bring Your Good Ideas to the President hours, Mark felt that he could structure his open-door time more efficiently in a way that forced people to display their own expertise when they came to him.

2. Since Mark was president of the Council of Industries and had a specific agenda for Commerce Bank at the council, he did not want to delegate this community obligation to Alex. But to avoid protracted meetings, Mark implemented his small group of experts process at the Council of Industries. He recognized that, for the process to work, he would need a strong executive director at the Council, and he hand-picked chairpersons for action-oriented subcommittees. Mark could then serve as a balance wheel encouraging the subcommittee chairper-

sons to act and making sure that they wouldn't move unless they had a good chance of success.

Note that if Mark had given the Council of Industries assignment to Alex but had maintained strict oversight over Alex's work in order to pursue his own agenda, he would have violated both Alex's pattern and his own. Alex's pattern required freedom from expectations and no pressure to do the project in any way except his own, and Mark's pattern required him to work together with others only as needed in a loosely structured way, not strict oversight. Because the Council of Industries agenda was important to him, Mark retained the assignment, but he restructured it so that it fit his pattern better.

3. Finally, Mark noted that he could identify unused capacity in his key employees and send them to training programs to build the bank's capacity for future action. To measure the success of this in-house training, he could invite key employees to tally their new ideas.

These negotiations between Alex and Mark, which were based on the ways of working that their patterns had indicated would be most successful, resulted in a division of responsibilities that fit the pattern of each man. They both found that their working relationship improved dramatically.

General Principles

When you work with two people who have widely divergent patterns, you are much more likely to find a way to divide a job so that different aspects are assigned to each person. Because any such division reflects the balance of power within the situation, many theoretically possible ways of working automatically have to be rejected. The best approach is to get the two people together and have them share and explain their patterns. When they do, points of conflict and disagreement become immediately obvious, which greatly simplifies the task of communication. Once they identify the salient and beneficial differences between them, they can collaborate on appropriate divisions of work that minimize their conflict and take advantage of their different strengths. There is almost always a way.

17

Suggesting New Ways to Divide Tasks

THE CASE OF THE TWO PARTLY EFFECTIVE PLANT MANAGERS

Organizations can grow up with an internal structure that has its own logic but that does not fit the people in it. This structure resists change because no one in the organization has ever known anything different. The logic seems convincing because it is familiar, and that prevents those operating in the environment from stepping outside to see an alternative. Even when a newcomer, such as a new manager, sees a more effective way of structuring operations, broaching the subject to those accustomed to the prevailing structure can be problematic. To make matters worse, if the structure seriously limits the organization's effectiveness, people tend to absolve the structure (if they even think to examine it for weakness) and blame themselves and their own shortcomings for the problems that they see.

Some managers who see a better way act to force change. But that is highly disruptive, and it can cause resentment that does not go away. If restructuring is not essential to improve performance, managers simply learn to live with the awkward arrangement. Often, some minor quirk in the system actually justifies the existing structure. And past attempts to replace it created new problems that no one had anticipated. After this happens once or twice, nobody wants to take the risk.

In scenarios like these, High Performance Patterns can help everyone see the convincing logic of change. They help to personalize a needed systemic change. A manager who uses patterns to initiate even the most obvious organizational change will find that the process goes much more easily, because subordinates are already convinced that it's the right thing to do.

Management Team Reorganization

Henry Marks was named manager of a midwestern paper mill owned by Rogers & White, a major manufacturer of brand-name goods in the United States and Europe. This plant had the worst record in the company for customer service: only 75 percent of its orders were filled on time (that is, within seventy-two hours), and only about 75 percent of the time did the customer actually receive what he or she had ordered.

Henry had initiated a major drive to improve customer service. After a year, the plant had improved significantly on the two indices: both stood at the low 90 percent level.

To continue this progress and facilitate the next leap in plant improvement, the entire management team took our high-performance workshop together. They discussed the results—their individual High Performance Patterns—at their next regular weekly management meeting and drew the implications that they saw for their own operation.

"When our plant managers became aware of their High Performance Patterns, it provided them with a way to propose changes that would make the group of us more effective and that everyone could understand because the changes were connected to our individual differences," said Henry. "Every manager looked at performance-improvement ideas from the new perspective of individual High Performance Patterns. I also talked with each individual on the management team about the work assignments or adjustments that seemed more in line with his or her pattern."

Senior Managers Propose Changing Their Jobs

The most dramatic effect that our seminar had was on Dan Timic and Roger Welsh, the plant's two production managers (one level below Henry). After the seminar, they proposed a radical shift in their responsibilities based on their own patterns. In effect, they proposed to have Roger take over Dan's job so that the plant would have only one production manager and to put Dan on special assignment to look for improvement projects "to make money for the company," as director of a think tank–skunk works at the plant.

"As their manager," Henry explained, "I could see how well the new proposal fit them both. From the moment I arrived at the plant, Dan and Roger were about as opposite as could be. Dan was an extremely popular, high-energy manager who loved bounding about his half of the plant, shaking hands, calling people by name, listening to everyone's ideas about what they could do to make something better, encouraging them to try it, and giving impromptu funny 'rewards' to people over lunch hour. He wanted to be on the plant floor. If it was up to him, he'd eat lunch with his people.

"Not surprisingly, Dan hated being stuck in his office doing the careful planning and statistical work necessary to keeping a production operation highly efficient. He did it, but his heart wasn't in it.

"Roger, in contrast, was reserved, aloof, difficult to get to know even at his warmest. He loved production planning and statistical control and preferred working in his office. He'd eat lunch there, alone, if he could. He disliked walking the plant. He did it and managed to make it work, but it was always awkward. Mostly he hated having to answer questions on the fly when he hadn't thought out his answers fully."

Henry went on to explain that he had often mused about how to restructure the jobs of his top two people so that Roger's skills and strengths in planning and control and Dan's strengths at innovation and morale building could be used throughout the plant. But such a restructuring would have been unusual and difficult to implement. The company divided all plants of this size in half and had a different person running each half. As might be expected, Dan and Roger did not get along well. Their respective halves of the plant were rivals.

The kernel of the breakthrough was actually planted at the workshop when we paired Dan and Roger in an exercise. As each man listened to the other's High Performance Pattern and one of his high-performance stories, there was a moment of revelation. Roger asked incredulously, "You mean you like wandering around the plant talking

High Performance Pattern for Dan Timic

1. I constantly read, study, attend conferences, and enroll in additional training to stay aware of cutting-edge technical and social concepts while looking for ideal situations in which people would be receptive to the new approach and in which we all could gain a huge success if it works.

2. I translate the cutting-edge concept into a personal vision of a change that would improve the situation and the lives of all the people in it.

3. I talk formally and informally with everyone who would be affected to share and focus the vision, typically using my enthusiasm and general sense of competence to convince them that they can do this and really benefit from it.

4. I identify the key strategic events and time them so that execution will move us significantly toward the vision, explaining to people why we need it to be done this way.

5. I delegate the details and execution of the daily key factors to people in the situation whom I have come to trust as a result of our interactions about the plan and the vision, often giving lots more responsibility to people than they ever had before or expected to get.

6. I check, study, talk, listen, backslap, refine, and/or redefine what we do to take advantage of what we learn as we go and to keep technology and people in balance.

7. I see people grab hold of the process and let them run with it, helping them through the rough spots but basically encouraging them to solve the problems they encounter.

8. I act as if I have the license to pursue the activity wherever it goes, the more complex the better, even if the real payoff won't come until the long term, in order to push the thinking and performance of us all.

9. I end up being seen as an expert in cutting-edge technology and being able to point to hard measures of improvement in technology and in people's results and satisfaction.

High Performance Pattern for Roger Welsh

1. I notice or I am made aware of a difficult, urgent situation and initiate work on it immediately, going directly to it and gathering as much live information I can.

2. I identify the elements that are key in making the system or situation function effectively, producing a kind of interactive model of how it ought to work.

3. I bring in experts and people in the situation to broaden and clarify the issues, until I think I have a good fix on what's wrong.

4. I present this picture of the situation for review and ask for solutions that allow the work to proceed and resolve the problem. I continue to press everyone responsible until a good solution emerges.

5. I establish boundaries, guidelines, expectations, and time lines for getting the solution into place so that no one backs off from full commitment to correcting the problem.

6. I establish review points and opportunities for further input, so that everyone knows when he or she will be held accountable and when good ideas for refinements or improvements will be carefully considered.

7. I facilitate, listen, and ensure that issues are worked out at each review point, leaving no problem lingering and no good idea unexamined.

8. On completion, I give feedback, recognition, and rewards to the people who have worked the hardest and contributed the most to building on and improving on our original solutions.

9. I receive personal recognition for the results from others who panicked at the original crisis and who really appreciate the cool and disciplined way I brought it under control.

to people and answering their questions?" Dan was equally surprised: "You mean you like sitting in your office working on careful production schedules and plowing through statistics?" From that moment on— given the context of the workshop, which emphasizes learning to use the strengths of people different from yourself—they each saw a way of getting out from under the parts of their jobs that they detested—by trading.

This insight opened the door for Henry to broach the subject that he had long been mulling over, how to make better use of their respective strengths. They proposed the restructuring themselves, which allowed Henry to implement it without incurring suspicions of hidden motives. "The wisdom of the shift was so clear in Dan's pattern and Roger's pattern," Henry explained. "Dan's pattern is about finding innovative things and getting them going. To limit this to the particular division that he managed was a real loss. Roger had the perfect pattern for managing the operations of the entire plant because he monitored everything very carefully, planned carefully, and dealt with deviations from statistical norms or unplanned breakdowns in production processes."

To understand how their High Performance Patterns helped this shift in responsibilities make sense, we looked at Dan's and Roger's patterns.

Dan's pattern confirmed and enriched Henry's observations of him over the few years they had worked together. In general, patterns confirm direct experience, but they enrich it by adding explicit detail about the way in which the person's success process works. In this case, Dan could see that the excitement and satisfaction for him came from putting some cutting-edge concept in place, training people, and then watching them use the concept to make great improvements in their results. He also enjoyed being seen as the expert in the concept. No wonder he didn't like production planning or statistical control. His pattern was about pushing the envelope of the possible.

Roger's pattern, as you can see, is about implementing rigorously controlled improvements, typically in response to some obvious problem. He models the key factors, determines what needs to be fixed, demands that a solution be found, and then stays on top of the process until the solution is implemented. No wonder he likes production planning and statistical control. They are tools for squeezing more performance out of an existing system that quickly identify deviations from the optimal and rapidly enable problems to be corrected.

Selling the Proposal to Company Management

"The plant had matured since the first job assignments were made. New systems were in place, and two people were no longer really needed as production managers," said Henry. "But Rogers & White is very cautious about such changes. They want to see very explicitly who's accountable for each piece of the operation and how lines of accountability are shifted. What I had to do was set a framework of accountability around Dan's and Roger's proposal that would allow me to sell it to my boss."

Everyone on the plant's management team supported the proposal. Dan had been responsible for customer relations and for a portion of planning for customer service that included warehousing, transportation, and distribution. Roger had responsibility for the engineering side of the operation as well as for quality assurance and another portion of the planning. The plant management team agreed that it made no logical sense to keep these functions separate, and that one person—Roger—could handle them all.

Since Dan was motivated by cutting-edge ideas, the idea emerged to have Dan start a think tank–skunk works at the plant. That would give him license to roam the plant looking for ways to improve things, getting improvement projects under way and motivating the people involved until they succeeded.

To get approval, Henry needed to ensure that the skunk works team would be held accountable for results that would improve plant performance. Dan was confident that he could continue and expand his history of innovation for the company. He had no problem being held accountable for his results. In its final shape, his assignment was to come up with ways of making significant amounts of money for Rogers & White that did not require new capital investment. It was his ideal arena: helping workers improve what they did.

Dan created a skunk works with six of the brightest people at the plant. It was the first Rogers & White plant to have one. They made two rules: Everyone had to sign every report that came out of the think tank, and everyone had to be in the office between 10 A.M. and 2 P.M. to optimize communication. Otherwise, they were free to be anywhere in the plant, working on whatever they could get going.

Under Dan's direction, the group took a fresh look at the whole issue of plant design. How could they maximize the efficiency of the company's capital investment? They came up with a model that would reduce downtime when the texture or color of the product was being changed. With their model, incremental improvements could be made at existing plants that would have a large cumulative effect over time. At the end of the first year, they prepared a report showing over $100 million in potential savings simply by doing routine things at the plant in new ways. The report became the basis not only for new plant design at Rogers & White, it became a model toward which every plant could move. From then on, the company justified every innovation and every capital investment by the degree to which it moved a plant toward this ideal model.

Roger had always wanted an opportunity to run the entire production and customer satisfaction end of the plant, since it was the only part of a Rogers & White plant that he had never run. He was so experienced at operations that he continued to run his section of the plant successfully while undertaking his new responsibilities. By the time he retired two years after the job change, the plant's on-time and as-ordered indices were up to 99 percent.

Discussing the Undiscussable

As Henry described it, the High Performance Patterns helped the management team discuss possibilities that would otherwise have been difficult to broach, because they enabled people to see in written form why a particular shift made sense for the persons involved. They then had more confidence that the change would work when it was implemented. Not only did each person find the act of identifying his or her pattern motivating and enlivening, the ease with which people could talk about what they needed in order to do their best work was a real gift.

From a general manager's point of view, patterns help in a number of ways. First, they confirm what you already know about your people, such as what Henry had observed about Dan and Roger. As a manager, you need not fear that patterns are going to surprise you. Although they do provide detail about why certain behaviors work for certain people, they will confirm your general observations and knowledge of your people.

Second, patterns make it possible to discuss possibilities that people might have viewed with great suspicion if they were tendered out of the blue. It is easy to get a whole team of people to brainstorm about how to use each person most effectively once everyone knows each person's pattern. Out of that interaction come many possibilities for working together more effectively.

18

Using Patterns to Change the Focus Within a Group

THE CASE OF THE UNIVERSITY PRESIDENT AND HIS MISASSIGNED BOARD

Experienced managers know that effective management requires treating each employee as an individual, figuring out the kinds of assignments, rewards, and supervision that will bring out his or her best. High Performance Patterns simply enhance this process by improving its accuracy, speed, and completeness.

As a manager, it is well worth your effort to learn to use your employees' High Performance Patterns to get better work out of them. Patterns are written in natural language. Each person develops his or her own pattern. Thus patterns give employees a natural bridge that enables them to explain how they can do an assignment best and which assignments are right for them. Such communication enables managers to help employees be successful.

Most managers can learn fairly soon how to interpret patterns and discuss them with employees to improve their performance and thus their own effectiveness as managers. They find that patterns confirm what they have already guessed or know from experience about their employees, and patterns are very helpful in guiding clear communication.

It is quite another thing to derive the patterns by interviewing employees. Applying already written High Performance Patterns and deriving a pattern through rigorous analysis of a person's set of high-performance stories are rather different. The second process is not simple. Even when one has developed the skill of finding patterns, that skill degrades rather quickly if it is not used frequently. We practice rigorous quality control to ensure that our trainers and consultants stay up to speed in discovering patterns. Such control is essential. Even our own skill drops if we are not careful. In most cases, it is simply not cost-effective to have a manager learn how to find patterns. It is better to use experts for the one-time discover-the-pattern process and then train managers and employees to use them. We tell companies to consider the initial cost of discovering the pattern an investment in its people. You have to invest a certain amount of time and money to find the patterns. Once the patterns are known, employees and managers can use them again and again to produce sustained high-performance results in assignment after assignment.

The case described in this chapter demonstrates that it is possible to learn to discover patterns and that it can be done to great benefit even when the power relationships are inverted. However, the person who did it, a licensed psychologist and the author of a number of books, was already skilled as an interviewer and counselor. He came to the task with a significant amount of prior experience with his own pattern and with related expertise. In this case, he used patterns to maximize the efficacy of the board of regents of the university that he headed.

First, some background. The relationship between the president of a nonprofit organization and his or her board is often difficult. While the board wields real power, its members are volunteers, often wealthy individuals, whose interests in serving on the board need to be nurtured. Any tasks that they are asked to perform have to be significant. The energies of board members can be quite destructive if they are not channeled productively. Executive directors and presidents manage such channeling as best they can, but the information at their disposal is often limited. They pretty much let board members decide what to pursue. Knowing board members' High Performance Patterns can greatly simplify the process of channeling their strengths.

In the case that follows, I worked with a university president whose background and training had made him highly skilled in interviewing and pattern recognition. He had considerable knowledge of our methodology, and the power relationships between him and the board made it awkward to suggest or require that his board members attend our workshop or work with me individually. For this reason, I had him collect the high-performance stories from his board of regents in the process of his regular meetings with them. Then I helped him discover their High Performance Patterns. I stayed in close touch with him as he gave the individual patterns back to board members, discussed them, and used them as a springboard for discussions about board assignments. As a result, he and board members made a number of adjustments in responsibilities that served them all well.

The Case of the Misassigned Board

When psychologist and academician Art Noble was appointed president of Thomas Jefferson University, he knew his High Performance Pattern. Indeed, he had used it in deciding to take the position. He worked best when dealing with long-standing problems in human development that seemed to defy solution. Many of his significant contributions to scholarship involved the development and active dissemination of detailed prototype solutions to enduring educational problems.

Jefferson University had been founded twenty years earlier as an unconventional university offering working adults a wide range of degree programs in such fields as law, management, liberal arts, psychology, and counseling. The school, which had a solid reputation for both academics and practical course work, required the active participation of its board of regents for fund-raising and administrative support.

After a frustrating series of interactions with Jefferson's board of regents and with considerable evidence that some were interfering with the university's healthy functioning, Art decided to use the regents' High Performance Patterns—and his own—to determine the best role for each member.

Finding a more effective way of working with Jefferson University's board fit Art's pattern well. The problem was a long-standing one that had resisted a satisfactory resolution throughout the university's twenty-year history. Some of the founding board members were still

High Performance Pattern
for Art Noble

1. I choose to deal with a long-standing problem that violates a deeply held value of mine and that has defied a definitive solution.

2. I obsessively collect and master all existing knowledge about the problem and existing solutions to the problem until every new source reconfirms what I have already learned.

3. I run through endless mental scenarios until I have developed clear criteria for recognizing a better, simpler, more effective solution to the problem as a whole and to the intermediate solutions that must be addressed along the way.

4. I act using my initial, trial solutions, imposing my values on the situation in such a way that the people in the situation have to respond on my terms, but in the least confrontational way possible, escalating only if I have to in order to get a response.

5. I find that my initial actions do not work, which creates frustration, a sense of failure, and increased determination to find a way through.

6. I buy time and quit actively working on the problem until I either see a pattern forming that makes the problem solvable or I simply can't wait any longer.

7. I gather the means and complete a prototype with obsessive focus on details so that it will be as close to perfect as possible.

8. I make sure that the prototype solution is disseminated (published, given away to others who will use and develop it, and so on) and actively engage in teaching others what I can about how to apply what I've learned to their situations.

9. I leave the problem, cherishing the success and the feeling of liberation from it.

on the board twenty years later and in a certain sense considered the university to be their own plaything.

True to his pattern, Art set out to master the situation. He came from a very strong value position in seeking to solve this problem. As he put it to the board, "It is very clear to me that a kind of administrative efficiency is possible when you know the special talents of the people you work with. It goes well beyond what we think of as merely efficient or effective administration. As we teach each other about our High Performance Patterns, we can define our roles in ways suited to our unique talents, and we can work in complementary ways that will best serve Jefferson University."

In order to define the patterns of Jefferson's board of regents, Art started by meeting with each regent separately to interview him or her about past successes—times when results came easily and things went so well that it almost seemed like magic. Each board member told three success stories. For each story, Art carefully inquired about how the person had gotten involved, what he or she had done to get things going well, what kept things going, and what ended the process. He made careful notes. The whole process was fascinating for him.

Despite the fact that he had a Ph.D. in psychology and long experience in interviewing people, he had never focused only on success stories or on what had worked for a person. Instead, his training had focused on looking for what didn't work and on attempting to get the person to change.

He and the regents found the meetings to be among the most meaningful that they had ever had. They felt an instant and close bonding. It became easy to explore possibilities, and they found that they could talk about some long-standing dissatisfactions with their roles that no previous president had been open to hearing.

Working with me, Art listed what he saw as the similarities within each person's set of stories. For each regent, we ended up with a pattern statement of eight or ten elements that told how he or she did his or her best work. Art edited the patterns a second time in one-on-one meetings with individual regents. For each regent, he developed a pattern statement that the regent agreed was his or hers and expressed in his or her own language.

Changing Roles on the Board of Regents

Art described the process from that point on: "We could see that we had people with unique talents, and we had often put them on committees that left them no way to do what they did best. As I listened to people's stories and examined the patterns that we found, I began to think that the best way of maximizing the energy and expertise of our regents was to have a whole series of special assignments that allowed each person to get involved with the university by doing something that was tremendously important and useful to it.

"So we shifted our focus, reducing the emphasis on regents' meetings and committee meetings and increasing the emphasis on having regents participate actively in projects for the school."

The next three sections describe three such reassignments. In each case, we supply enough about the person's pattern to indicate why it made so much sense.

Assignment: Creating a Maverick Position for the Chairperson

The high-performance stories of businesswoman Ramona Washington, who chaired the nominating committee, revealed that she had extraordinary talent in meeting important people and getting them to do things for her, often at considerable inconvenience. Her three stories told of wangling an invitation from Pablo Casals to tour with him and his orchestra; tracking down the chairman of a major corporation and getting him to come down off the slopes at Vail for a meeting; and deciding one morning in India to meet Mother Theresa, succeeding in arranging the meeting, and spending the afternoon with her at her mission.

But Jefferson was not using Ms. Washington's talent for making contacts and planning extraordinary encounters. Instead, she was stuck with extensive administrative work associated with the job of chairing the committee. Art recommended that she relinquish the committee chair position, a recommendation that she enthusiastically supported. He asked the board to appoint a chairperson who was skilled at facilitating meetings and who could assume those functions when the nominating committee was convened. Between Art and Ms.

Washington, they identified a number of types of individuals that the university needed, and she became his search leader.

Assignment: Evaluating Computer Systems

Allison Sommers, one of the university's founders and a brilliant data analyst, had been assigned to Jefferson's finance committee. Her stories showed that she was at her best working with masses of data that she could analyze on her own. She was attracted by the task of putting together her own way of understanding something complex.

As a member of the finance committee, this preference proved a constant thorn. No matter how much effort the university staff put into it, she always found fault with their analyses or the way they had put data together. She was constantly redoing the financial information that the board received and arguing that the board should use her analysis, not that of the staff. Although she meant well, her behavior was demoralizing for the staff and divisive for the board. Of course, she could not understand why everyone didn't just accept her results as the better solution. Art wanted a different assignment for her but one that she would be motivated to accept.

The breakthrough came when we realized that her impressive financial analysis skills didn't limit her pattern to financial data that could be run on a computer. In a broader sense, her pattern was about making sense of complex data, more often messy qualitative data than merely financial.

Since Jefferson needed to select a major computer system for the university's next decade, Art suggested that Allison take charge of the selection process. When he presented this idea to her and used her pattern to justify it, Allison was delighted. This would give her her own project. It had great value for the university, and it would free her from what she saw as constant nitpicking and whining from the staff.

In her new assignment, she researched requirements, interviewed computer users and department heads to establish needs, gathered information on three competitive computer systems, and made a recommendation that won approval and accolades from the board for its thoroughness and convincing criteria. Her work saved the university the cost of a $70,000 needs assessment. For the whole project, she was doing just what she liked to do. Her rededication to the board and her remotivation were striking.

Assignment: Starting a New Eldercollege on Campus

Another of the university's founders, law professor Mark Addison, was a prolific contributor to the regents. But for years, as a member of the committee on academic matters, he had called every staff policy decision into question, which was demoralizing for the staff and the other members of the committee. Honored and respected for his immense contributions to the founding of the university, no one wanted to challenge him directly. Nevertheless, his attempt to run university policy was inappropriate and destructive, particularly since the university was now large and complex.

Mark's stories demonstrated that he took a strong interest in starting new ventures, particularly when he had identified a need and knew nothing about the details of how to get such a project going. For example, besides having been absolutely pivotal in getting the university started, he had organized a highly successful career development center on campus that had become a national model.

Based on Mark's stories and pattern, Art simply asked Mark to identify the needs that he saw now at Jefferson university. Mark reported that he had heard of a program for senior citizens that focused on preserving renewable resources for grandchildren. He thought it would be a great thing to get started on the campus. Moreover, it might attract many more of the elderly to become university students, a growth market that the university was positioned to serve.

When Art replied that it was a great idea and asked why didn't he pursue it, Mark protested that he didn't know anything about it. Then Art pointed out that, according to Mark's pattern, not knowing anything was one of the factors that had always motivated Mark. He agreed, and Art recommended that he take responsibility for planning a new Eldercollege for Jefferson University. Mark undertook the project with great enthusiasm, which eliminated his attempts to intervene in the daily running of the university.

General Principles

"The advantage of working with patterns is that we start by looking at what has worked for each person, and we celebrate his or her strengths by helping the person to do what he or she likes and does best," Art explained. "When each member of a group works in a way that is compatible with his or her own pattern, it also creates an intensely strong kind of connection among the members of the team, because everyone likes doing his or her work well and everyone likes working together successfully."

As a general rule, written patterns help bring people back to what is really important for them and to what they really want to do. If possibilities for new assignments are brought up, people characteristically look for hidden agendas and wonder why someone (Art, in this case) wants to change what they do. When the pattern is there to support and justify the change, the discussion assumes a very different tone. Each person can genuinely explore whether the proposal would in fact be the best thing, without suspicion or second-guessing. Patterns make decision making much easier.

19

Answers to Typical Questions About Applying Patterns to Pairs

As the examples in Part III have shown, the same principles that were applicable to individuals govern situations involving pairs and groups. The objective is to find a way for people to function together that works for each person, that truly honors individual differences, and that uses those differences in positive ways. It is astonishing how often a way can be found that does work perfectly even when the two people dislike each other and have never been able to work together amicably.

If in reality there is an effective way of working together, the key is to uncover it. This requires a way to cut through the negative projections and conclusions of both parties. High Performance Patterns address this need in a way so distinct from any of the standard communication and listening techniques that our process often succeeds when nothing else has.

From the outset our underlying principle—honor each other's High Performance Pattern absolutely—acts as a safety net. Each person knows going into the negotiation that the outcome will not require one to change in order to accommodate the other. Each participant has already gone through the process of finding his or her pattern, which reinforces our fundamental principle. Each has already come individually to trust the consultant and the procedure.

Our procedure requires each participant to understand the other's best way of working. Listening to the other describe his or her way of working and asking questions about it can break down barriers to cooperation based on false assumptions and attributions. Participants are often able to recognize the value in many seemingly negative aspects of the other's way of working when they can see those aspects in the context of the entire success process. This first step toward conflict resolution informs the negotiation that follows.

Once the participants are familiar with each other's pattern, they must scrutinize the values on which they base their relationship. When the underlying values have been aligned in some fashion, the specifics regarding how to cooperate in a particular activity become less important. Because most business situations are predicated on an implicit agreement to collaborate for the collective success of the team, department, or company, achieving an alignment based on shared values is relatively simple. It is not necessarily as simple in personal situations, but we still find that, in the vast majority of cases, people who want to work together share a large number of values.

Next, our process requires the parties to examine their complementary roles and capabilities. These are often numerous. Virtually anyone in virtually any situation can see ways in which the different capabilities of others can improve their collective chances for success.

Finally, by the time we address the actual points of conflict, the pair already has built a very strong foundation on which to base a viable solution, at least for the current activity. A solution is almost always possible when it needs to last only for the duration of this activity. We never insist or expect two people in a business relationship to end up life-long friends as a result of our process. We do expect them to find a way of making necessary cooperation a value-added experience.

Having outlined the process, let me answer some of the questions that people often raise.

1. *Doesn't it take a long time to find and apply patterns for two or more people?*

As with the individual process, the amount of time needed is relative. How much time is lost because two people who need to work effectively together don't like each other? The negative side effects are enormous. How do they weigh in the balance against the few hours it takes to negotiate a viable solution? In the case of Dan and Roger, half the plant had squared off against the other half because the two managers didn't work well together. No wonder their results were so poor. In each case involving pairs or groups described in this section of the book, the cost of the time wasted far exceeded the cost of finding the patterns and sitting down carefully with each pair to work out effective ways of cooperating.

2.   *When does it not work?*

No process can solve the problem of getting two people to cooperate if they really don't want to. Sometimes we find people who are really into zero-sum games. They figure that only one can win, and each wants to win—at the expense of the other if necessary. The corporate mythology about the value of competition is still strong, although company after company is recognizing how ultimately destructive it is. When a pair refuses to find a way to cooperate, particularly if there are obvious ways they could cooperate that they reject, we suggest that they stop pretending. We run into this situation most in nonbusiness settings. Business settings entail real sanctions for individuals who can't get along, no matter how competent they are.

3.   *Aren't there times when the levels of competence are so different that cooperation as if the two people were equals doesn't make sense?*

Yes. That principle was operating in the bank case. The CEO was far more effective at running the bank than the chairman, so whether the chairman could even be considered one of his "experts" was at issue. Yet even there, neither individual was going to go away. They needed to find a way of making the best of it. When they adopted that perspective, they found ways of using the chairman's talents, although these may have been less numerous than the CEO would have preferred. In general, even if one person in a pair is clearly the junior partner, minimizing conflict is still important. Differences in levels of skill and experience never justify putting the lower-level person in a circumstance in which he or she can't produce his or her best work.

4. *Isn't one or the other partner in a session often skeptical that the other's pattern really is what is written down?*

Yes, of course, though since each has been through the process, there is also considerable trust of the written pattern. Sharing one or more of the stories helps. More commonly, in problematic relationships, each person may have never seen the other truly "on pattern." They have a history of experiencing each other's negative behaviors. They both need to go through a period of time in which they stay on pattern and grow to trust each other's willingness to do so, instead of taking advantage of each other.

5. *How important is a third-party consultant to helping pairs of people work out beneficial accommodations?*

It depends how serious the impasse. In many cases of mutual good will, the process of sharing patterns and finding better ways to work together is exciting and energizing. A consultant's role is simply one of making sure that points are heard and of encouraging deeply creative possibilities.

In more problematic relationships, the consultant plays an important initial role of structuring the discussions so that the two do not fall back into old patterns of mutual dislike and distrust. The structured process described at the beginning of Part III controls the interaction and makes it positive. The consultant actively enforces the process. Often, of course, the ones who most need a third party are most reluctant to use one. We recommend always using one for the first session.

CONCLUSION

The Unique Advantages of High Performance Patterns

Having spent this much time and effort to understand the technique of High Performance Patterns and the process used in working with them, you may recognize the patterns as a next-generation technology. The characteristics of High Performance Patterns make them useful and beneficial in the following ways:

- They are written in natural language. You don't need to be an expert to read or interpret them.

- They are derived from a straightforward empirical analysis of examples, not through intrusive delving into the psyche.

- They have a broad range of application—planning, problem solving, choosing among alternatives—in situations ranging from huge organizational issues involving thousands of people to one-on-one demarking of personal goals and directions.

- They can be used over and over again; they are not just a one-shot phenomenon.

- They are of lasting value; patterns remain stable for years.

- They are universal; everyone has one, regardless of age, education, experience, gender, ethnicity, or economic opportunity. Everyone has the capacity to improve his or her performance significantly, no matter where he or she begins.

- They provide an individual model for the whole process of achieving success, not just for one personal trait or characteristic.

- They describe and guide the individual through a personal success process step by step, not merely providing general traits of a static category of people.

- They point the way to fast and nondisruptive resolutions to seemingly intractable problems.

- They break down barriers to communication and make it possible to integrate newcomers quickly into complex tasks.

- They build personal confidence and trust in one's own instincts and judgments.

- They explain the importance and limitations of imitation and recipe-following to reach competence while showing how individuals can go beyond mere competence to outstanding performance.

- They distinguish grind-it-out processes, which lead to short-term peaks and burnout, from sustained high-performance processes, which yield far greater results in the long run.

- They simplify and shorten the creative struggle to find better ways of working in complex, messy situations.

- They provide a communication vehicle to develop mutually beneficial ways of acting when two or more persons are involved. In particular, they encourage the easy discussion of options that might otherwise be considered "undiscussible" or too loaded to bring up and consider openly.

- They identify, use, and build on what already works rather than presenting idealized general models that do not fit.

- They help people act responsibly in complex and rapidly changing situations and thereby reduce the need for close supervision.

- By confirming what is already known, they lead to ways of acting that people recognize as right and true when such lines of action were not apparent through other techniques.

- They help people to value traits and behaviors that they regarded as personal weaknesses by showing how such behaviors work in the individual success process viewed as a whole. Patterns enable people to recognize their undervalued strengths.

- They suggest a natural style of leadership to any individual.

- They leave no lingering regret or guilt, even when the best efforts fail.

- They serve deep-seated values and provide a context for creating meaning and purpose out of action in complex realities.

- They connect a good idea to the driving energy of an individual who can serve as its champion.

- They show how to honor differences.

- They demonstrate that being true to oneself makes room for others to be true to themselves.

Although the list of benefits just sketched is impressive, even more important substantive conclusions can be drawn from our work with High Performance Patterns. These conclusions are evident from the few examples shared in this volume.

First, *we all are unique and different*. It's not just something that we wish were true.

Second, *our unique qualities are the essential elements of how we produce our best work*. They aren't trivial or something that we want others to acknowledge grudgingly. We need other people to celebrate our special qualities and help us give them full expression, and we need to do the same for them.

Third, *it is relatively easy to find a way of expressing our pattern that fits the constraints and the purposes of the organization context in which we work.* High Performance Patterns help us achieve optimum expression in a positive and value-added way and help us avoid the compromises that diminish our effectiveness. There is always some way both to be on pattern and to fit the situational constraints without compromise.

Fourth, *staying true to a pattern and seeing where it leads often produces a novel idea or a niche product that the organization has overlooked.* Honoring patterns stimulates out-of-the-box thinking and a perspective on organizational sacred cows that is fresh yet practical. Empowerment isn't just a good idea or some abstract principle. It is the operating process by which we can bring the full capabilities of a work force to bear on making the organization work.

Fifth, *by describing the full process of becoming successful, not just one characteristic or behavior, patterns make it possible for people to collaborate and share responsibility without getting in each other's way.* The rich uniqueness of the full process of becoming successful gives others lots of opportunity to use their full processes too.

Finally, *High Performance Patterns and the process of using them are uniquely American.* As a culture, we embody and celebrate individualism probably more than any other culture. Rather than imitate Japan, for instance, which has a deeply ingrained group culture, or France, which has a deep distrust of collective action, Americans have needed to develop a unique methodology that brings the unique strengths of American culture to bear on our problems and opportunities. High Performance Patterns have such promise. They show how we can tie individual uniqueness to group purposes without compromising either in a way that no other technique does.

In their groundbreaking research on High Performance Patterns, professors Robert Quinn and Gretchen Spreitzer (Quinn, Spreitzer, and Fletcher, 1992) describe patterns as the process by which people make meaning of their lives and their environments. The high-performance stories on which patterns are based represent people's ways of understanding their importance in their organizations. The management literature contains various typologies of meaning-making mechanisms and behaviors, but High Performance Patterns suggest why it is so important that we understand such mechanisms.

The following quote by Quinn and Spreitzer will bring home their main points (Quinn, Spreitzer, and Fletcher, 1992):

> *Management theories have traditionally focused on general theories and prescriptions to the neglect of individual meaning systems. Organizations are structured to be organic or mechanistic, integrative or segmentalist. Managers are autocratic or participative. Jobs are designed for the "average" individual. Yet, findings from the analyses in this paper suggest that each individual is driven by different needs, searches for meaning through different paths, and manages different paradoxes and tensions. . . . Thus these findings suggest that a generalized management approach may not be appropriate and may actually be dysfunctional for high performance behavior.* (p. 26)
>
> *An understanding of individual meaning systems also has implications for individual empowerment. A critical component in the process of empowerment is the development of a sense of purpose or meaning. Empowered individuals feel a sense of personal meaning and seek to discover ways to attune that meaning with higher levels of organizational purposes.* (p. 27)

To other consultants handling the human side of organizations and change, I offer this suggestion: It has been obvious to those of us who have worked with various personality typologies and category schemes that eventually we needed to work at the level of the unique individual. But how to handle the resulting complexity when we work with an organization? Categorizing people in some fashion has seemed essential, so we have compromised what we really knew to be necessary.

The way to a real solution is to step farther into exactly what we thought was impossible. Using High Performance Patterns, I have found that it is genuinely possible to empower people. When we give them insight into how they do their best work and when we celebrate their unique individuality, it becomes easier to manage the variety and complexity of the capabilities needed to produce outstanding results, not harder. Our work with individual High Performance Patterns has pushed through to the individual level. The results are what we always hoped they would be.

It may seem anticlimactic for me to remind everyone at the very end of this book that the truth isn't in the technique. But it isn't. When we engage with a person to identify his or her High Performance Pattern, we engage to help the person find what seems to be true for him or her about how he or she is successful in the world and to help the person see it in a way that is genuinely helpful and empowering. Techniques help. Being well trained in a particular technique is essential to disciplined work. Yet it is precisely the discipline that enables us to transcend technique when we do our best work. We are seeking insight for the person, not a platform for our methodology. Anyone who finds the approach described in this book persuasive should have the same motivation.

I can say that, as change becomes increasingly rapid and as companies downsize, reorganize, and redeploy people almost constantly, a motivated, purposeful, and flexible work force is essential. Such a goal can be achieved only through individual self-knowledge and personal development, not by manipulating external rewards and disincentives. The act of uncovering one's own individual High Performance Pattern is like throwing out a sea anchor in a storm. It gives a person a chance to regain his or her bearings in the storm of change and make positive moves even in the face of great uncertainty. It is truly a technology for our time.

REFERENCES

Bolles, Richard N. (1990). *What Color Is Your Parachute?* Berkeley, CA: Ten Speed Press.

Haldane, Bernard. (1974). *Career Satisfaction and Success: A Guide to Job Freedom.* New York: American Management Association.

Jung, Carl G. (1977). *The Portable Jung.* (J. Campbell, ed.) New York: Penguin Books.

Kiersey, David, and Bates, Marilyn. (1984). *Please Understand Me.* New York: Prometheus.

Kouzes, James M., and Posner, Barry Z. (1987). *The Leadership Challenge.* San Francisco: Jossey-Bass.

Peters, Thomas J., and Waterman, Robert H., Jr. (1982). *In Search of Excellence: Lessons from America's Best Run Companies.* New York: Harper & Row.

Quinn, Robert E., Spreitzer, Gretchen M., and Fletcher, Jerry L. (1992). "Excavating the Paths to Meaning, Renewal, and Empowerment: A Typology of Individual High Performance Myths." School of Business Administration, University of Michigan, Ann Arbor.

(A much more extensive and highly personal bibliography on high performance is available from the author.)

INDEX

THE AUTHOR

Jerry L. Fletcher has had a lifelong fascination with the process by which more or less ordinary people come to do things outstandingly well.

Majoring both in the hard sciences (physics and mathematics) and in history, Jerry received his bachelor's degree in the history of science from Harvard. There he developed a deep respect for the way in which systematic bodies of thought develop and come to be accepted.

After two summers of teaching in Africa, Jerry became intrigued by the relationship between values and action, between what people said they believed and what they actually did in the real world when confronted with the need to act. Since two of the outstanding professors in this field were at the Graduate School of Education at Harvard, Jerry continued his studies there, where he earned his doctorate. His dissertation dealt with simulations and games as teaching devices. He was also a founding member of the editorial board of the *International Journal of Simulations and Games*.

In the mid seventies, as one of two senior policy analysts in education for the federal Department of Health, Education, and Welfare, Jerry began to explore every approach he could find that purported to enable people to reach very high levels of achievement. In the process, he chaired national conferences on the outer limits of human perfor-

251

mance and became nationally recognized as an expert in the dissemination of innovations.

In 1979, Jerry left the federal government to found a company that would pursue what had become his fascination with outstanding human performance. He began working one on one with highly successful individuals who wanted to become even more successful. He soon discovered the powerful links between an individual's uniqueness and his or her process for achieving results. The conclusion: Each person's route to outstanding performance involved learning to make use of his or her own uniqueness. This conclusion flew in the face both of theory and of conventional wisdom, which proposed that the path to success was to imitate other successful people.

Within several years, Jerry had developed a process whereby individuals could identify the specific actions that they took and the conditions that were present when they achieved their best work—their High Performance Patterns.

Now, more than a decade later, Jerry's company, High Performance Dynamics (HPD), has become a leader in the field of human performance and in handling the human consequences of large-scale organizational change. HPD's client list ranges from such large corporations as IBM, Digital Equipment Corporation, Procter & Gamble, and Monsanto to hundreds of smaller companies and to individuals. The company's data base contains more than five thousand High Performance Patterns, the largest data base of its kind in existence. The company has also developed an innovative team-building approach based on discovering and utilizing the unique strengths and qualities of team members. This program is finding wide acceptance in cross-functional, self-directed, and goal-specific teams.

Jerry is also a trained improvisational comedy actor—a skill that has stood him in good stead in the consulting business—and he was the straight man in a comedy company that performed political satire in Washington, D.C.

Jerry lives with his wife Kathleen and their seven-year-old daughter Cassie. If you would like to talk with him to pursue any of the ideas set forth in this book, you can reach him at High Performance Dynamics, 56 Woodside Drive, San Anselmo, California 94960. His phone number is 415-456-5200. The fax number is 415-454-1560.